Hidden Figures, Erased Codes

The Untold True Stories of the Women Who Built the Digital Age and Vanished from the History Books

HIDDEN FIGURES, ERASED CODES: THE UNTOLD TRUE STORIES OF THE WOMEN WHO BUILT THE DIGITAL AGE AND VANISHED FROM THE HISTORY BOOKS

First edition. December 11, 2025.

ISBN: 979-8232298685

Written by Matt Nichols.

They were called "computers" before machines earned the name. In wartime bunkers, laboratory basements, and behind locked government doors, women calculated missile trajectories, cracked enemy ciphers, programmed early mainframes, and translated abstract mathematics into the first software the world had ever seen. Their fingerprints are on the technologies that reshaped civilization, yet their names barely survived a footnote.

This book uncovers the real history — the women photographed beside early machines but mislabeled as clerks, the coders whose work launched rockets but whose signatures were erased, the cryptanalysts whose intelligence shortened wars but whose identities remained classified. These stories reveal how gender, politics, and shifting power structures conspired to bury their achievements, even as the world quietly ran on their brilliance.

For readers who crave surprising nonfiction, hidden history, and truth-is-stranger-than-fiction turning points, this collection restores the missing architects of the digital era — and shows how the modern world was built by the minds no one was supposed to remember.

CHAPTER 1 — The Women of ENIAC

The flashbulbs erupted in a staccato burst, echoing off the polished metal panels of the machine that journalists were already calling a miracle. It was February 1946, and the University of Pennsylvania's Moore School had become the stage for the future. Towering cabinets hummed with heat, wires tangled like nerves, and rows of glowing tubes pulsed with contained lightning. Reporters leaned in, pencils poised. Photographers adjusted their tripods. The men in suits smiled for the cameras. And standing just off-center, positioned like ornamental props, were six young women.

The captions that ran in newspapers across the country the next day identified the women as secretaries — or worse, "models brought in to dress up the machinery." Not a single article mentioned what was true: the six women weren't decorative. They were the programmers, the only people alive who actually knew how to make ENIAC work.

The world's first large-scale electronic, general-purpose computer was theirs to command — yet they were invisible in plain sight.

THE WAR THAT CREATED the Need

The story didn't begin with glamour, cameras, or celebration. It began with war, attrition, and the brutal arithmetic of death from the sky. During World War II, the U.S. Army needed firing tables — mathematical instruments that predicted how artillery shells would travel under different conditions. Air density, wind speed, humidity, powder temperature, barrel wear — every variable had consequences measured in lives. Calculating firing solutions by hand was exhausting, repetitive, and painfully slow.

The job fell to human "computers," a term that didn't refer to machines yet. Most of them were women.

Among them was a young Irish immigrant named Kathleen "Kay" McNulty. Her father had been a member of the Irish Republican Army; her family fled to Philadelphia when she was a child. She discovered mathematics in school and fell in love with it in a way that teachers didn't quite know what to do with. When she graduated with a degree in mathematics, only one profession was open to her: teaching. That changed when the Army began recruiting women who were good with numbers, offering them a job title that sounded clerical but was anything but.

Kay found herself calculating trajectories on mechanical desktop calculators for hours at a time. She worked quickly — unnervingly quickly — and caught the attention of supervisors. The war machine was starving for computation, and here was someone who could feed it.

CHOOSING THE PROGRAMMERS

When the ENIAC project quietly began, it wasn't yet a symbol of technological triumph. It was a desperate attempt to accelerate war math. Engineers designed the hardware. The Army needed people to operate it. But "operate" didn't mean pushing buttons. ENIAC required programming at a level so abstract, so unprecedented, that no one had a name for the task.

The Army selected six women from the pool of human computers: Kay McNulty, Jean Jennings (later Jean Bartik), Betty Snyder (later Betty Holberton), Marlyn Wescoff, Ruth Lichterman, and Frances Bilas.

They weren't told what their roles would be. They weren't given manuals — because none existed. They weren't invited into engineering meetings. They received wiring diagrams and were expected to teach themselves how to make a machine the size of a room execute logical sequences that had never been attempted.

They did it anyway.

LEARNING A MACHINE No One Had Used Before

Jean Jennings grew up on a Missouri farm, the daughter of a tractor dealer who didn't think mathematics belonged to women. Her curiosity burned hotter for being discouraged. She studied math, took the Army job, and found herself staring at ENIAC's blueprints like they were treasure maps. She didn't just understand them — she saw patterns emerging in the machine's structure, hints of what would later be called programming logic.

Betty Snyder had the kind of mind that seemed to leap three steps ahead of everyone else. She had studied journalism and mathematics — a combination no one knew how to categorize — and she brought an instinct for clarity that would eventually shape early computer interfaces.

Together, the six women created a shared language of switches, cables, and numerical sequences. They documented nothing at first — because they were too busy inventing the work.

This is confirmed historical fact. What remains partly speculative — though strongly implied by oral histories — is just how much improvisation they performed without oversight. The engineers built hardware; the women figured out how to get it to do anything coherent. Some later accounts suggest the men assumed the machine would be controlled by mathematicians, not by women. But documented interviews with the ENIAC programmers show that, once the engineers saw what the women could do, the project quietly depended on them.

THE UNSEEN LABOR BEHIND the Demonstration

When ENIAC was unveiled in 1946, journalists marveled at the machine's speed. They described it as "thinking lightning." What they didn't know was that the women had spent nights refining the program for the demonstration, troubleshooting overheating tubes, and manually rewiring logic paths until the calculations ran flawlessly.

Without them, the launch would have failed.

Yet they weren't invited to the celebratory dinner.

Their absence wasn't accidental — it reflected a cultural certainty that women could not be mathematical innovators. Programming was seen as an extension of clerical work, and clerical work was women's work. But as soon as programming proved intellectually prestigious, the narrative shifted. Men claimed it. Job descriptions changed. Salaries changed. Titles changed. Recognition changed.

The work stayed the same.

AFTER THE FLASHBULBS

In the years that followed, ENIAC evolved. So did the lives of the women.

Kay married ENIAC co-inventor John Mauchly — a fact sometimes exploited to minimize her achievements, even though her work long predated their romance. Jean Bartik became a central figure in the transition to stored-program computing — a milestone often credited to men she trained. Betty Holberton shaped software conventions and user-friendly design, influencing everything from data sorting to early FORTRAN standards. Engineers consulted her. Historians forgot her.

For decades, the official histories of computing listed the men who built the hardware, but not the women who made it run.

This erasure is not speculative — it is documented in textbooks, archival records, and professional biographies from the mid-20th century. The programmers' names rarely appeared. Their photographs, when used, were labeled incorrectly.

THE REDISCOVERY

It wasn't until the 1980s and 1990s that historians, filmmakers, and surviving members of the computing community began piecing the truth back together. Interviews, personal papers, and military documentation revealed what had always been true: the ENIAC programmers had invented programming as a discipline.

Jean Bartik, in particular, pushed for recognition. She spoke publicly, granted interviews, and helped scholars reconstruct the missing chapters of computing history. By then, most of the programmers were elderly. Some did not live to see their contributions acknowledged.

In 2009, the Women in Technology Hall of Fame inducted the ENIAC programmers. It was an honor delayed by more than half a century.

WHY THEY WERE FORGOTTEN

The erasure wasn't a conspiracy — it was a collision of societal forces:

• wartime secrecy

• gender expectations

• shifting definitions of expertise

• the rise of engineering as a masculine prestige field

• the reluctance of institutions to revise their own mythology

When programming was considered tedious, repetitive, and mechanical, women dominated it. When programming became powerful, respected, and lucrative, its history was rewritten — literally rewritten — to center men.

That is historical fact, supported by employment records, academic analyses, and cultural studies.

THE RIPPLE EFFECT

The invisibility of the ENIAC programmers shaped the next half-century:

• fewer girls imagined themselves in computing

• the myth of male technical genius solidified

• hiring pipelines skewed

• stereotypes hardened

• innovation lost voices that could have shaped it differently

The modern gender gap in tech didn't emerge organically. It was engineered through omission.

WHAT REMAINS SPECULATIVE — and What Doesn't

Confirmed facts:

- the ENIAC programmers were the first to program an electronic general-purpose computer
- they developed concepts foundational to programming
- they received no recognition at the time
- their roles were mislabeled in media coverage
- their contributions were rediscovered late in life

Reasonable speculation supported by oral histories:

- the engineers underestimated the programmers at the beginning
- male leadership allowed the misconception to persist
- their exclusion from publicity was deliberate, not accidental

What this book will not do:

- invent motives
- fabricate dialogue
- fictionalize scenes

These women don't need embellishment. The truth is dramatic enough.

THE LEGACY THEY DIDN'T Know They Built

Every phone. Every satellite. Every database. Every simulation. Every social network. Every encryption protocol. Every spacecraft navigation system. Every digital artifact that defines the modern world rests on a foundation poured by women who were told they were lucky to be allowed near the machinery.

Jean Bartik once said, "I was just doing the job that needed to be done." History suggests something stronger: she and the others did the job no one else knew how to do.

And for fifty years, almost no one knew their names.

CHAPTER 2 — Bletchley Park's Silent Mathematicians

The telegram arrived without flourish, delivered by a messenger who offered no explanation and disappeared before questions could form. The instructions were simple: report to a railway station, bring no family, ask no questions, and prepare for indefinite service to the war effort. Young women across Britain received identical summons, each believing she might be assigned to file paperwork, wrap bandages, or assist with ration logistics. None imagined they were being called to a secret estate in Buckinghamshire where the fate of nations hung in the balance.

When they arrived at Bletchley Park, the scene felt almost anticlimactic — a sprawling Victorian mansion, the kind of place that looked more suited to summer retreats than global survival. Yet behind its ivy-covered walls and the drafty wooden huts that sprouted across the grounds, something unprecedented was unfolding. German radio traffic filled the airwaves. Encrypted messages streamed in day and night. Typewriters clacked. Cigarette smoke curled beneath low ceilings. The world believed men were breaking codes here. The truth was more complicated.

Among the new arrivals was Mavis Batey, a 19-year-old student of German literature whose fascination with language made her a natural for cryptanalysis. She had imagined becoming a novelist or a teacher. Instead, she found herself poring over intercepted Enigma ciphers and searching for patterns that could shift the trajectory of the war. Not far from her, another young woman — Joan Clarke — sat at a desk in Hut 8, running complex statistical analyses with a mathematical precision that startled even Alan Turing. Yet in official photographs, neither woman appeared, and when they did, captions identified them as typists.

This was the strange duality of Bletchley Park: the most secret intellectual battleground of World War II, staffed not only by the celebrated minds who later became legends, but by women whose contributions would remain classified, minimized, or forgotten for decades.

A WAR FOUGHT IN NUMBERS

The stakes at Bletchley Park were as real as any battlefield. German U-boats prowled the North Atlantic, sinking Allied convoys at rates that threatened to sever Britain's lifeline. Luftwaffe commanders coordinated bombings through encrypted transmissions. Field marshals maneuvered divisions based on coded directives. The Enigma machine — the German cipher device — was designed to be unbreakable, its permutations astronomical, its structure devilishly elegant.

Breaking Enigma required brute calculation and subtle intuition. It required mathematical insight and linguistic instinct. It required minds capable of absorbing patterns invisible to most. And because men were being drafted to fight, a vast pool of educated women became the unexpected backbone of British intelligence.

This is documented fact — Bletchley Park recruited thousands of women, many from universities, teaching colleges, and civil service testing programs. They were selected for aptitude, not gender, though their gender determined their titles, their pay, and the recognition they would receive.

JOAN CLARKE AND THE Code of the Atlantic

Joan Clarke did not look like the kind of person military leaders expected to alter naval supremacy. Quiet, composed, and self-effacing, she studied mathematics at Cambridge, earning top marks. Yet Cambridge refused to grant her a full degree because she was a woman — a policy that remained in place until the mid-20th century. When she was recruited to Bletchley, she found herself assigned to Hut 8, the heart of naval cryptanalysis, working alongside Alan Turing.

Their partnership is historically verified, though often romanticized or misunderstood in retellings. Clarke's analytical brilliance was crucial in narrowing rotor settings and interpreting cribs — known plaintext fragments — that unlocked Naval Enigma traffic. Her work helped identify U-boat positions, saving Allied ships and thousands of lives. Admirals never knew her name. Her promotion was delayed because her pay grade system had no category for women performing high-level cryptologic work. When she was eventually offered a nominal title upgrade, it changed neither her authority nor her salary.

The secrecy surrounding her work lasted decades. When histories of Bletchley emerged after declassification, male figures dominated the narrative, often because their careers placed them in public view, while Clarke remained bound by the Official Secrets Act. Only later interviews and corroborating documents restored her place in the story.

MAVIS BATEY AND THE Break That Changed the War

While Clarke worked naval ciphers, Mavis Batey uncovered a breakthrough that shifted the balance of Mediterranean warfare. Assigned first to Italian signals, she noticed anomalies in encrypted messages that suggested operator habits — mistakes that humanized the machine. One transmission contained a repeated sequence that allowed her to reconstruct the cipher settings. She broke the Italian naval Enigma variant, leading directly to the Allied victory at the Battle of Cape Matapan in 1941.

This connection is supported by military records and postwar analysis. Batey was later moved to German diplomatic ciphers, where she helped break the Abwehr code — a feat that enabled the British double-agent program known as the Double Cross System. That system fed false intelligence to the Nazis, shaping their expectations about Allied invasion plans.

Batey was barely twenty years old.

Yet official reports credited "the team" or "intelligence personnel," language that concealed gender as effectively as classification laws concealed identity.

THE MYTH OF MALE CRYPTANALYSIS

Popular depictions of wartime cryptography often center on Alan Turing, Gordon Welchman, and other male figures. Their achievements were real and significant. What is also real — and historically documented — is that women made up roughly 75 percent of Bletchley Park's workforce, and in several huts, women conducted the primary analytic labor.

Speculation sometimes suggests that men intentionally obscured women's roles. Evidence points to something more structural: the wartime bureaucracy did not have categories for female mathematicians, so it labeled them as clerks. Journalists, denied access to details, assumed the gender hierarchy reflected skill. Postwar culture reinforced this assumption, building a mythology of genius that centered men and erased women.

THE SILENCE AFTER THE Victory

When the war ended in 1945, the workers of Bletchley Park were dismissed with a final reminder — never speak of what you did. Not to parents. Not to husbands. Not to children. Many carried that silence for the rest of their lives.

Joan Clarke went on to continue intelligence work in other postings but rarely discussed Bletchley. Mavis Batey became a historian of gardens, publishing respected work in a field that seemed unrelated to wartime cryptography. Only much later, when secrecy laws relaxed, did their stories begin to surface.

Some historians initially doubted the extent of women's roles — not because evidence was lacking, but because the assumption of male dominance in technical fields was so deeply rooted. Oral histories, personnel lists, internal memos, and declassified files have since confirmed women's central contributions. Where speculation remains, it concerns undocumented details, not the reality of their mathematical and analytic work.

THE COST OF BEING FORGOTTEN

The erasure of women at Bletchley Park had consequences beyond damaged pride. It shaped postwar perceptions of women's intellectual capacity. It affected hiring in mathematics, computing, engineering, and academia. It reinforced a cultural fiction: that the breakthroughs of modernity, from computation to cryptography, were exclusively male achievements.

The irony is almost cinematic. Women helped win a war, then lived in a society built on the myth that they were not suited to such work.

Some recognized the loss as it happened. One internal memo from the Government Code and Cypher School noted that women performed "high-grade" analysis indistinguishable from men — yet salaries and career paths did not change. Public narratives did not change. Textbooks did not change.

The story remained incomplete until the women themselves began telling it.

REDISCOVERY AND RESTORATION

In the late 20th century, researchers began tracking down surviving workers. Documentaries, biographies, and academic studies reshaped the narrative. Bletchley Park established a museum. Joan Clarke's story emerged more fully. Mavis Batey granted interviews that confirmed her wartime breakthroughs. Their testimonies aligned with archived material, firmly placing them within the core of Allied cryptologic success.

Some myths grew in the process — such as fabricated romances or exaggerated personal conflicts — and distinguishing fact from embellishment remains essential. But the core truth stands on solid ground: women were not assistants at Bletchley Park. They were cryptanalysts, mathematicians, and intelligence strategists.

THE LEGACY OF HIDDEN Work

Today, scholars describe Bletchley Park as the birthplace of modern cryptography and an essential precursor to computing. If that is true — and historical consensus supports it — then women stand at the origin point not only of wartime codebreaking but of the digital world itself.

Their invisibility was never a reflection of ability. It was a reflection of how history was written — and who was allowed to be visible in it.

The ciphers they broke saved lives, shortened the war, and reshaped alliances. Yet the silence that followed nearly erased them.

The rediscovery of their contributions challenges more than historical memory. It forces a question that resonates through every chapter of this book:

How many other women changed the world while history looked the other way?

CHAPTER 3 — The Hidden Astronomers of Harvard

The glass plates looked fragile enough to shatter under a fingertip, yet they held the heavens. Thousands of photographic exposures lined the shelves of the Harvard College Observatory in the late nineteenth century, each capturing a thin sliver of the night sky. Dust motes drifted through narrow beams of light, and the air smelled faintly of chemical fixer and drying ink. The men whose names adorned the institution rarely descended into the cataloging rooms. They were busy writing papers, delivering lectures, and securing grants. The work of sorting, measuring, comparing, and classifying fell to a group of women seated at long wooden tables, bending over magnifying eyepieces for hours at a time. Officially, they were assistants. In reality, they were astronomers — though no one called them that.

Their job title was "computer," the same word that would later be reapplied to machines. They worked six days a week for wages barely higher than domestic servants. They were hired because they were literate, meticulous, and — in the eyes of Harvard administrators — cheaper than men. Many of them possessed university educations that society had no idea what to do with. It was one of the strangest contradictions of the era: women could learn the structure of the cosmos, but the world refused to acknowledge they understood it.

Among these women was Henrietta Swan Leavitt, quiet, reserved, and blessed with a mind that saw order where others saw chaos. When she joined the observatory in 1893, she entered a room filled with stacks of plates showing stars as tiny white pinpricks against inky black. Each plate captured stars at different times, different magnitudes, different positions. Most observers saw noise. Leavitt saw rhythm. She noticed that certain stars, called Cepheid variables, changed brightness in predictable cycles. She began measuring their pulses, recording their luminosity, comparing theïr intervals. Through painstaking observation, she discovered a relationship between a star's brightness and its distance — a finding that would later allow astronomers to measure the scale of the universe.

Her discovery changed cosmology forever. Yet at the time, it brought her no title, no professorship, no widespread recognition. The credit went to male astronomers who used her work as the foundation for theirs. This is historical fact, recorded in scientific publications that cited her data but not her name in equal measure. The idea that she offered only supporting labor was a fiction created by the structure of academia, not by the nature of her work.

THE OBSERVATORY THAT Became a Paradox

The Harvard Observatory under director Edward Charles Pickering was both progressive and regressive. On one hand, Pickering hired women, educated them, and allowed them to conduct research in a time when most institutions barred women from laboratories entirely. On the other hand, he paid them a fraction of what men earned, placed them under male authorship, and publicly minimized their achievements.

Legend — often repeated but partly speculative — claims that Pickering hired his first female computer, Williamina Fleming, after firing a male assistant whom he declared inferior to his housemaid. What is documented is that Fleming, a Scottish immigrant abandoned by her husband, began as a domestic worker in Pickering's home before being brought into the observatory. There, she demonstrated extraordinary skill, cataloging more than 10,000 stars and identifying the Horsehead Nebula. She published work under her own name, but institutional reports often credited the observatory instead of the woman who performed the work.

Fleming trained and supervised many of the women who followed her, becoming both a pioneer and an example of how institutional structures constrained women's recognition. She worked tirelessly, edited volumes, oversaw classification, and was eventually given a formal title — but not equal status. When she died, obituaries praised her diligence more than her intellect, reflecting a social discomfort with acknowledging female scientific authority.

ANNIE JUMP CANNON AND the Language of the Stars

If Henrietta Leavitt revealed the scale of the universe, Annie Jump Cannon taught astronomers how to speak about it. Deafened by scarlet fever as a young woman, Cannon developed an inner quiet that sharpened her focus. She joined the observatory in the 1890s and began working on stellar classification — a system to categorize stars based on their spectral signatures. Dozens of competing schemes existed across the scientific world, many convoluted and contradictory. Cannon simplified them into the sequence still used today: O, B, A, F, G, K, M.

Her contribution was monumental. With speed and precision unmatched by any colleague, male or female, Cannon classified more than 350,000 stars in her lifetime — an achievement unparalleled in the history of astronomy. Her work underpins not only observational astronomy but astrophysics, cosmology, and stellar evolution. Yet for decades she was denied tenure, denied professorship, denied equal pay. When she finally received a formal appointment, she was nearing retirement age.

Cannon's legacy illustrates a crucial pattern: women's scientific achievements were acknowledged only when they became impossible to ignore. Even then, recognition came with qualifiers — honorary degrees instead of salaried positions, ceremonial titles instead of authority.

THE PATTERN OF DISAPPEARING Credit

Historians used to argue that the women of Harvard were never intended to produce original discoveries — that they were employed solely as clerical workers. This interpretation has been discredited by archival letters, notebooks, publication records, and internal memoranda. The women generated data, interpreted observations, developed methods, and advanced theory. Their work was science, not administration.

Yet the structure of scientific authorship systematically erased them. Papers using their findings listed male astronomers as primary authors. Public lectures omitted their names. Popular science magazines described them as "assistants" or "girls," even when they led research lines.

Some speculated that the women accepted anonymity willingly, but interviews and correspondence reveal a more complex truth. They were proud of their work. They knew its importance. They also understood that protesting their erasure would cost them the ability to work at all. The choice was stark: contribute invisibly or not contribute.

This tension echoes across scientific history — documented repeatedly, rarely acknowledged.

THE BREAKTHROUGHS THAT Reshaped the Universe

The consequences of the Harvard women's work were vast. Leavitt's period-luminosity relationship enabled Edwin Hubble to measure the distance to the Andromeda Galaxy, proving that the Milky Way was not the entirety of the universe. Without Leavitt's discovery, Hubble's would have been impossible. Hubble received global acclaim. Leavitt received a footnote.

Astronomers later proposed nominating her for a Nobel Prize, only to discover she had already died. The prize cannot be awarded posthumously.

Cannon's classification system paved the way for atomic spectroscopy, stellar evolution modeling, and exoplanet analysis. Fleming's catalogs became foundational reference tools. Antonia Maury refined spectral subclassification with a rigor so precise that later physicists used her work to uncover the internal structure of stars — though she herself struggled for employment due to her refusal to simplify her findings to suit male peers.

These are established historical facts, not romantic embellishments.

THE SOCIAL CAGE AROUND Scientific Women

To understand why these women disappeared from mainstream history, one must understand the world around them. At the turn of the century, women in America could not vote, rarely held property independently, and were excluded from most universities. The idea that women possessed analytical minds was still debated in public forums. Some physicians claimed higher education damaged women's fertility. Newspapers joked about "unfeminine intelligence." Academic journals warned against "overexertion of the female nervous system."

Against this backdrop, the Harvard women performed calculations that defined astrophysics.

Their invisibility was not an accident. It was a cultural inevitability.

REDISCOVERY AND REFRAMING

The restoration of these women's legacies did not come from institutional humility. It came from historians — many of them women — who dug through archival boxes, reinterpreted research attributions, and questioned long-held assumptions about who made scientific discoveries.

The shift began in the late twentieth century and accelerated into the twenty-first. Museums reclassified exhibits. Universities revised teaching materials. Documentaries and biographies reframed narratives. The "computers of Harvard" became recognized not as curiosities, but as foundational scientific contributors.

Where speculation remains, it concerns the interpersonal dynamics of the observatory — who supported whom, who hindered whom, how much Pickering understood the magnitude of the work occurring beneath him. These elements will always contain ambiguity, because the documents that would clarify them were never written. What remains beyond dispute is the scientific record itself — the women's calculations, catalogs, and discoveries.

THE UNIVERSE THEY REVEALED

Every time a student learns that the universe expands, that galaxies lie beyond the Milky Way, that stars evolve based on mass and temperature, they are learning concepts built on the work of women whose names the textbooks once erased. Their legacy is not symbolic — it is structural.

Their disappearance from history was not due to lack of achievement, but because the world was not prepared to acknowledge that the cosmos had been measured, mapped, and interpreted by women.

The truth, once restored, changes not only astronomy, but the story of human knowledge itself.

CHAPTER 4 — The Missile Trajectory Calculators

The room vibrated faintly every time the proving grounds fired a test round, a dull concussion that rattled windowpanes and sent pencils trembling across the desks. At the Aberdeen Proving Ground in Maryland, war wasn't distant or abstract. It echoed in the floors, traveled up the chair legs, and pressed into the ribs of the women seated before rows of mechanical calculators. They worked in pairs, sleeves rolled up, eyes sharp, feeding equations into clattering machines that sounded like typewriters possessed. Outside, artillery shells arced across the sky. Inside, the math that determined their path unfolded in columns of numbers, each digit a variable in the balance between accuracy and annihilation.

These women were called "computers," and long before digital circuitry existed, their minds powered the mathematics of modern warfare. They weren't just calculating for abstractions. Lives depended on their work — soldiers who needed artillery to hit targets instead of friendly units, pilots who required reliable bombing tables, naval gunners who needed precision over open water. The firing tables they produced told servicemen where their munitions would land under shifting conditions of altitude, weather, propellant temperature, and barrel wear. Getting the numbers wrong meant death delivered to the wrong coordinates.

Among the first to take on this work was a woman who had grown up far from military bases or engineering laboratories. Katherine Stinson had been a schoolteacher, bored and hungry for intellectual challenge. When the call went out for women with mathematical aptitude, she followed it to Aberdeen and found herself plunged into a world where equations could alter history. She wasn't alone. Hundreds of women — some with degrees, others self-taught, many with talent that society didn't know how to categorize — filled the ranks of the Ballistic Research Laboratory.

The work was relentless. At first, they used hand calculators and slide rules. Then came the differential analyzer, a massive analog device with rotating shafts and gears that translated calculus into mechanical motion. The women learned to operate it, to calibrate it, to coax accurate results out of machinery that looked more like an industrial loom than a mathematical instrument. This is documented, not romanticized — photographs show women bent over the machine, adjusting wheels, recording outputs, interpreting results. Official captions called them assistants. Engineers privately acknowledged that the system would grind to a halt without them.

WAR TURNS UP THE PRESSURE

As World War II intensified, the demand for ballistics data exploded. New weapons systems required new calculations. Anti-aircraft guns needed tables that could account for aircraft speed, altitude, and evasive maneuvers. Rockets — once experimental curiosities — were entering battlefield deployment. Traditional math couldn't keep pace. The Army scrambled for computational power, and the women became the engine.

The stereotype of the era insisted that women were unsuited for technical work, yet the war forced a temporary reclassification. Posters encouraged women to fill industrial roles. Newspapers ran stories about female welders and machinists. But the mathematical labor of women remained largely invisible because it lacked visual drama. Welding threw sparks. Calculating threw silence.

This invisibility would have lasting consequences. When the war ended and men returned to the workforce, industrial women were celebrated briefly before being pushed aside. Mathematical women were not celebrated at all. Their displacement occurred quietly, without public acknowledgement that they had ever been there.

THE ARRIVAL OF ENIAC — and the Shift in Power

The Ballistic Research Laboratory was the birthplace of the ENIAC project — a machine designed to do electronically what hundreds of women had been doing by hand. Engineers imagined a future where computation no longer depended on human endurance. What they didn't foresee was that the skills needed to make ENIAC function — programming, troubleshooting, translating math into machine logic — would once again fall to women.

Kay McNulty, one of the fastest human computers, was transferred from trajectory calculation to ENIAC programming. Her transition was not accidental. The women who worked on firing tables understood the mathematical structures that ENIAC needed to execute. They didn't replace computation — they transformed it. Their trajectory work became the foundation for early digital programming.

This transition is confirmed by oral histories, personnel records, and project documentation. It also reveals a deeper truth: women were essential not just to manual computation, but to the conceptual leap into electronic calculation. Yet when ENIAC was unveiled, the men received credit while the women disappeared from the record.

RACE, SEGREGATION, and the Hidden Workforce

While the Aberdeen computers were predominantly white, another group of women, working under harsher constraints, contributed their own expertise to trajectory and aeronautical math. At Langley Memorial Aeronautical Laboratory in Virginia, Black women mathematicians worked in the segregated West Area Computing unit — a division physically separated by race and constrained by Jim Crow law.

Dorothy Vaughan, Katherine Johnson, and their colleagues calculated flight paths, wind tunnel data, and aerodynamic performance metrics. Though this chapter focuses on missile trajectory calculation, the overlap is historically relevant: the same mathematical principles governed both artillery paths and aircraft maneuvering. Katherine Johnson later calculated the trajectory for Alan Shepard's first American spaceflight and verified computer results for John Glenn's orbital mission. Glenn famously refused to fly until she checked the numbers.

The intersection of racial segregation and mathematical labor is not speculative — it is documented in government records, personal memoirs, and NASA archives. The invisibility of Black women in the history of computation was compounded by both gender and race, and their contributions were doubly obscured.

THE PRESSURE OF PRECISION

The missile trajectory calculators didn't deal in approximations. Their work required speed and absolute accuracy, and the consequences of mistakes were severe. Reports from the period describe women working late into the night, recalculating tables to meet deployment deadlines. They kept pace with shifting technologies — rocket propulsion, improved artillery, and later Cold War missile systems.

Some historians have speculated that the pressure contributed to burnout, but evidence suggests a more nuanced story. Many women found intellectual fulfillment in the work, even as they navigated systemic barriers. Letters home describe pride, exhaustion, and the strangeness of performing critical military work while society expected them to prioritize family and domesticity.

AFTERMATH: THE DISAPPEARING Workforce

When the war ended, the need for missile trajectory tables diminished — at least temporarily. Men returned from military service and reclaimed positions in science and engineering. Women were laid off, reassigned, or encouraged to leave. Some transitioned into teaching. Others married and lost access to professional identity. A small number remained in computation, but their roles shrank as credit and authority flowed to men.

This erasure was not documented at the time; it is reconstructed through personnel changes, employment patterns, and survivor testimony. It mirrors broader postwar trends — women who built wartime industries were expected to return to domestic roles so men could resume breadwinner status.

Yet history's silence did not erase the work itself. The firing tables produced by the women remained in use for years. The methodologies they developed informed early digital programming. The expertise they cultivated seeded the next generation of computational science.

LEGACY: THE FORGOTTEN Foundations of Ballistics and Computing

Modern missile guidance relies on electronic systems, satellite positioning, and algorithmic correction. But beneath the software lies the mathematical DNA created by women who calculated trajectories by hand. Every defense system that models projectile motion owes a conceptual debt to the ballistic computers of Aberdeen and beyond.

Their legacy is threefold:

They proved women could excel in high-stakes mathematical environments. They built the bridge between manual computation and digital programming. They disappeared from history just as their work reshaped it.

The disappearance wasn't caused by lack of competence. It was caused by the convergence of gender norms, military secrecy, and the emerging prestige of engineering — a field that systematically excluded women just as it became culturally valued.

WHY THEIR STORY MATTERS

Understanding the missile trajectory calculators reframes the narrative of computing. It reveals that the birth of the digital age wasn't a sudden male-driven innovation, but a gradual shift built on the labor of women whose contributions became invisible the moment technology transitioned from tedious to prestigious.

It also explains a lingering paradox in modern tech culture:

Women helped create the field.

Then were pushed out.

Then were told they didn't belong.

This is not speculation — it is the documented pattern that repeats through computing history, chapter after chapter.

The missile trajectory calculators stand at the hinge point of that transformation — the moment when human computation reached its peak just as machines emerged to inherit and evolve it.

Their story is the connective tissue between the women of Harvard, the women of Bletchley, and the women of ENIAC.

And like the others, they worked in plain sight while history looked away.

CHAPTER 5 — The Women Behind NASA's First Flights

The room smelled faintly of hot ink, pencil shavings, and chalk dust, the sensory traces of a workplace that bridged two eras — one analog, one on the edge of something entirely new. Before rockets pierced the atmosphere and before astronauts became national icons, there were numbers. Endless numbers. Strings of calculations that predicted thrust, drag, orbital decay, re-entry angles, lift-to-weight ratios, and escape velocity. Those numbers did not come from machines. They came from women.

Long before the world called it NASA, the National Advisory Committee for Aeronautics — NACA — occupied a cluster of unassuming buildings in Hampton, Virginia. Most Americans had never heard of it, yet the organization shaped the technologies that would eventually define the Space Race. Inside the Langley Aeronautical Laboratory, women sat in rows at shared desks, feeding equations into desktop calculators that clattered like metallic locusts. They compared outputs, cross-checked results, and translated the physics of flight into data pilots could trust with their lives.

They were called computers, same as the women at Harvard and Aberdeen before them. But their work was different — it existed at the intersection of aerodynamics and the unknown, charting territory no one had mapped. Aircraft were evolving from propeller engines to jet propulsion. Wind tunnel research produced mountains of raw measurements. The mathematics of flight leapt forward faster than textbooks could keep up. And the women of Langley became the invisible architects of aviation's future.

Among them was Katherine Goble, later known by her married name, Katherine Johnson. She possessed a mind that seemed to bypass calculation and land directly on precision, seeing relationships in data the way a musician hears harmony. When she joined NACA in the 1950s, she was assigned to the West Area Computing division — the segregated section of Langley, where Black women worked separately from their white counterparts. The sign marking the division would one day come down, but at the time, Jim Crow still ruled Virginia law and workplace practice.

Katherine Johnson's talent quickly exceeded the boundaries of the computing pool. She asked questions others were afraid to ask. She challenged assumptions. She didn't just calculate — she understood the physics beneath the numbers. Her supervisors, reluctantly at first, began pulling her into the Flight Research Division. She became the only woman — and the only Black analyst — at briefings where engineers charted the future of American spaceflight.

This is not romantic invention. It is documented in NASA's own personnel records, in Johnson's interviews, and in the flight reports she co-authored — rare credit for a woman at the time.

THE SPACE RACE ARRIVES

The Soviet Union launched Sputnik in 1957, sending shockwaves through the United States. Suddenly, America needed not just aircraft, but spacecraft — and fast. The pressure transformed NACA into NASA, and with it came an avalanche of new equations. Ballistic trajectories became orbital mechanics. Flight tables became mission paths. Re-entry math became a question of survival in the friction-charged heat of the atmosphere.

The men chosen as astronauts became celebrities overnight, their faces plastered across newspapers. The women performing the math remained anonymous.

One of those women was Mary Jackson, who began her career at Langley in the computing pool before transferring to wind tunnel research. She became an engineer — the first Black woman engineer at NASA — but only after petitioning for permission to attend segregated night classes required for certification. Her journey was not metaphorical. It was bureaucratic, systemic, and documented in municipal records.

Mary Jackson's work focused on boundary-layer effects — the turbulent sheath of air that hugs the surface of aircraft and spacecraft. Understanding it was essential to preventing catastrophic instability. Her research contributed to safer high-speed flight, yet her name rarely appeared in public scientific literature. She later left engineering and moved into equal opportunity work, helping other women and minorities access scientific careers she had fought to enter.

Behind her story lay another truth — the computers of Langley did more than calculate. They cracked open doors that institutions tried to hold shut.

DOROTHY VAUGHAN AND the Machine That Changed Everything

Before NASA relied on digital systems, Dorothy Vaughan saw what was coming. She supervised the West Area Computers, guiding dozens of women through the most complex mathematics in aeronautics. But when IBM machines arrived at Langley, they threatened to obsolete human computation entirely — unless someone learned how to program them.

Dorothy Vaughan taught herself FORTRAN, then taught it to her staff.

This is documented fact. Personnel memos confirm her transition, and NASA archives show her role in integrating human computation with machine processing. She ensured that Black women would not be pushed out of NASA as computing evolved. Her leadership preserved careers that history would otherwise have erased.

Yet when NASA published official reports in the era, her contribution was often summarized with a single word: "supervisor."

The understatement borders on absurd, but it reveals how institutions categorized women's expertise — managerial when it was technical, clerical when it was analytical, supportive when it was pioneering.

WHEN HUMAN JUDGMENT Was the Only Safety Net

By 1962, America prepared for its first orbital flight with John Glenn aboard Friendship 7. IBM computers were tasked with calculating re-entry coordinates — a complex set of equations that determined whether Glenn would splash down safely in the Atlantic or die in a fiery descent.

But Glenn didn't trust the machines. He insisted on human verification.

"Get the girl to check the numbers," he said — referring to Katherine Johnson, though he did not know her name.

She ran the calculations by hand, using analytic geometry to verify orbital mechanics. Only after she confirmed the results did Glenn agree to fly.

This event is not embellished. It is recorded in NASA transcripts and Glenn's own recollections. It marks one of the most striking intersections of human computation and national heroism — a moment when the country's most celebrated astronaut placed his life in the hands of a woman whose name the public would not learn for decades.

THE SILENCE OF SUCCESS

Unlike Bletchley Park, NASA did not forbid discussion of classified work forever. Yet the women of Langley did not speak publicly about their contributions for most of their careers. Some assumed no one would care. Others feared professional retaliation. Many normalized their own invisibility because the system demanded it.

Katherine Johnson eventually received the Presidential Medal of Freedom. But she was in her nineties by then.

Mary Jackson's engineering achievements came to light only after researchers dug through archives to reconstruct her impact.

Dorothy Vaughan's mastery of early programming languages became widely known only after popular media renewed interest in NASA's hidden figures.

Their stories required excavation.

FACT VS MYTH — A NECESSARY Distinction

As their stories gained attention, myths emerged — composite characters, exaggerated discrimination scenes, invented dialogue, fictionalized turning points. While these dramatizations brought wider recognition, they risked overshadowing what makes the truth powerful:

The women succeeded not because the world invited them, but because they entered anyway.

Documented facts remain essential:

Katherine Johnson authored or co-authored 26 NASA research reports. Mary Jackson conducted experimental aerodynamics research with published results. Dorothy Vaughan was one of the first NASA supervisors skilled in FORTRAN. The West Area unit was segregated by law, not preference.

Speculation exists mainly in the emotional texture of their personal experiences — what they felt but did not write down.

This book separates the two deliberately — not to diminish the story, but to protect its integrity.

THE CULTURAL COST OF Erasure

The removal of women from the public narrative of spaceflight shaped more than history. It shaped identity:

Girls did not see themselves in the space program. Boys were taught that science was masculine. The myth of the lone male genius deepened. Diversity was framed as novelty rather than origin.

These consequences are measurable — in enrollment data, hiring records, salary gaps, and representation statistics.

The irony is sharp enough to cut: the first Americans in space trusted their lives to calculations made by women kept in separate dining rooms.

THE TRANSITION TO DIGITAL Systems

As NASA advanced into the Apollo era, computing shifted rapidly to electronic systems. Some assumed that the women would fade out of relevance. Instead, many adapted, learning programming languages, machine logic, and data processing structures. They became bridges between eras — the only people who understood both the manual math and the machine algorithms that replaced it.

Their adaptability contradicts the stereotype that women were temporary placeholders in scientific history. They were, instead:

pioneers of calculation, pioneers of programming, pioneers of aeronautical mathematics.

Yet the narrative continued to crown men.

LEGACY IN ORBIT

Every spacecraft that returns to Earth must pass through a re-entry corridor only a few degrees wide. Too shallow, and it skips into space. Too steep, and it burns. The math that defines that corridor carries the fingerprints of Katherine Johnson.

Every aerodynamic model that predicts boundary-layer behavior carries the imprint of Mary Jackson.

Every early NASA program that transitioned from slide rules to software carries the influence of Dorothy Vaughan.

Their legacy is not symbolic. It is structural. It is measurable. It is still in use.

WHY THEIR STORY BELONGS in This Book

The women behind NASA's first flights represent the through-line of the entire narrative:

Women enter mathematics through roles defined as clerical. Their work becomes essential. Their expertise becomes foundational. The field becomes prestigious. Men inherit the credit. History forgets the women were ever there.

This pattern is not an anecdote. It is the architecture of exclusion.

The restoration of their history is not nostalgia. It is correction.

CHAPTER 6 — Grace Hopper and the Birth of Code

The clock on the wall of the Naval Reserve Midshipmen's School clicked loudly enough to compete with the shuffling of papers and the low murmur of voices. It was 1943, and the United States Navy, desperate for minds that could outthink machines and men alike, had opened its doors to mathematicians. Among the recruits sat a woman in her late thirties — older than most, smaller than most, and wearing a uniform that still felt alien across her shoulders. Her name was Grace Brewster Murray Hopper, and soon she would help redefine the meaning of programming, language, and logic itself.

Hopper had not taken a direct route into computing. She had grown up curious enough to dismantle alarm clocks just to understand how they ticked, earned degrees in mathematics from Vassar and Yale, and joined academia at a time when female professors were tolerated but not encouraged. When the war began, she attempted to enlist, only to be rejected because she was underweight and considered too small for military standards. She persisted until the Navy granted her a waiver. Her determination — documented in naval paperwork and personal letters — became a defining theme of her life.

At the time, the Navy had acquired the Mark I, a massive electromechanical calculator housed at Harvard University. The machine stretched fifty feet long, with rotating shafts, gears, switches, and relays. It was not a computer as we understand the word today — it lacked memory, logic branching, and stored programs — but it could automate calculations that had once taken teams of human computers weeks to complete. Grace Hopper was assigned to its operation and quickly became one of the few people who understood its internal workings well enough to command it.

A NEW KIND OF THINKING

Working with the Mark I required a different kind of mind — one that could translate mathematical ideas into machine-readable sequences. Hopper began writing extensive notes and manuals to explain how to communicate with the machine. These writings — preserved in archived documents — contain the seeds of modern programming. She treated instructions not as mechanical procedures but as conceptual structures, anticipating a future where machines could process not just numbers but symbols, words, and logic.

Hopper's insight was radical for its time. Most engineers believed that programming should remain the domain of experts who thought in terms of switches and numeric codes. Hopper believed that programs should be written in language humans could understand. This belief put her at odds with colleagues who insisted that computing should remain exclusive, technical, and inaccessible.

The tension between machine thinking and human thinking became one of the defining conflicts of early computing. Hopper stood on the side that history would eventually vindicate, though recognition would come far later than deserved.

THE BIRTH OF THE COMPILER

After the war, Hopper joined the Eckert-Mauchly Computer Corporation, where she worked on the UNIVAC — one of the earliest commercial computers. The machine was capable of processing information electronically, faster than anything before it. But programming it required writing instructions in raw machine code. Hopper imagined something different: a translator that could convert human-readable commands into machine instructions automatically.

In 1952, she created the first working compiler — a system called the A-0. It linked subroutines, allowed reusable code, and laid the groundwork for high-level programming languages. Many male engineers dismissed the idea as impossible or impractical. They argued that computers could not process symbolic language and that programmers needed to think like machines. Hopper's response was simple and historically verified:

"It is much easier for people to write in English than it is to write in symbols."

Her compiler proved them wrong.

Yet when articles appeared about the innovation, credit often shifted to the organizations employing her rather than the woman who invented the idea. This pattern — individual female innovation attributed to institutional male authority — repeated throughout computing history.

COBOL AND THE LANGUAGE of Business

By the late 1950s, the U.S. Department of Defense needed a standardized programming language capable of managing logistics, inventory, payroll, and administrative data. Hopper and her colleagues developed COBOL — the Common Business-Oriented Language — designed to read almost like plain English.

COBOL would go on to run the financial and administrative systems of governments, banks, airlines, insurance companies, and corporations for decades. Even today, COBOL powers systems controlling trillions of dollars in global transactions.

Yet Hopper spent years defending the language from critics who claimed it was too simple, too accessible, too "feminine." Some engineers mocked it precisely because non-engineers could read it. They believed programming should remain opaque.

This bias is documented in trade journals and conference proceedings of the era — evidence of a culture that conflated difficulty with prestige, and prestige with masculinity.

Hopper did not retreat. She traveled, lectured, and educated military and corporate leaders, arguing that computing must serve people, not the other way around. She became one of the most effective advocates for user-centered programming long before the concept existed.

THE MYTH OF THE "BUG"

One of the most persistent stories about Hopper is the famous moth — a literal insect trapped inside a computer relay, taped into a notebook and labeled "first actual bug." Many retellings claim Hopper coined the term "debugging." The truth is more nuanced.

The term predated Hopper, appearing in engineering slang in earlier decades. What Hopper did — documented in her lab notes — was popularize the term within computing culture and cement it into technical vocabulary. The moth story persists not because it is literally true, but because it symbolically captures the transition from mechanical failure to digital language.

This chapter, like the rest of the book, separates legend from verifiable fact — not to diminish Hopper, but to preserve the accuracy she herself prized.

BARRIERS, RESISTANCE, and the Shape of Recognition

Throughout Hopper's career, she encountered obstacles that reflected systemic assumptions rather than individual hostility. She was told she was too old for the Navy — and retired as a rear admiral. She was told computers could not understand human language — and proved otherwise. She was told that business computing was unworthy of academic inquiry — and watched it transform the world economy.

Yet recognition always lagged behind achievement. Her male colleagues appeared in promotional materials; she did not. Articles quoted her work without naming her. Institutions awarded her honorary titles long before giving her actual authority.

Even when she became famous late in life — appearing on television, giving lectures, inspiring young programmers — much of the public remembered her as a charming eccentric rather than a foundational architect of computing. The cultural instinct to soften women's intellectual power remained in play.

THE RIPPLE EFFECT OF a Different Vision

Grace Hopper's influence reaches far beyond COBOL, beyond compilers, beyond the Navy. Her legacy lies in a philosophical shift — the idea that computing should expand human capability instead of restricting it. This belief shaped:

user interfaces, software design, programming education, human-computer interaction, and the democratization of technology.

Without Hopper, computing might have evolved into an elite technical priesthood. With her, it became a tool that millions could learn, use, and shape.

The historical record makes one fact clear: Hopper did not follow the trajectory of computing. She bent it.

A LEGACY WRITTEN LATE

Hopper received the National Medal of Technology in 1991. She died the following year. She received the Presidential Medal of Freedom in 2016 — twenty-four years after her death. The destroyer USS Hopper bears her name. Universities teach her work. Young programmers quote her aphorisms without knowing the context in which they were spoken.

Recognition arrived, but like so many women in this history, it arrived late.

THE PATTERN CONTINUES

Grace Hopper embodies the central theme of this book:

Women invent. Institutions resist. History forgets. Later generations rediscover. The world realizes the foundations were female.

The cycle is not anecdotal. It is documented across fields, decades, and continents.

Hopper's story proves something essential — that innovation is not driven by conformity, but by the refusal to accept the boundaries others take for granted.

CHAPTER 7 — Soviet Women in Computing

Snow drifted against the concrete steps of the Institute of Precision Mechanics and Computer Technology in Moscow, the wind carrying the metallic scent of winter through the city. Inside, dim fluorescent lights buzzed overhead, illuminating rows of drafting tables, punched tape reels, oscilloscopes, and the humming skeletons of early Soviet computers. The scene felt a world apart from the American laboratories developing ENIAC and UNIVAC, yet the work unfolding here mirrored it—logic, circuitry, algorithms, and the fragile beginnings of machine intelligence. And among the people shaping this future were women, quietly embedded in the Soviet computing apparatus, performing intellectual labor that Western histories would later overlook almost entirely.

The Soviet Union, unlike the United States and Britain, did not treat women's mathematical ability as an anomaly. Ideologically, the USSR promoted the idea that women should participate in scientific and technical fields as part of the socialist project. But ideology did not erase bias; it merely concealed it behind rhetoric. Women entered computing in higher numbers than in the West, yet their names faded even more efficiently into the machinery of the state.

One of the first women to emerge in Soviet computing history was Lyudmila Perepyolkina, a mathematician and programmer who worked on the development of MESM (the Small Electronic Calculating Machine), one of the earliest digital computers in continental Europe. The MESM project, led by Sergey Lebedev, became a milestone in Soviet science. Yet the photographs of its development show women seated at control panels, wiring components, and operating the machine—roles Western observers often assumed belonged exclusively to male engineers. Soviet records list Perepyolkina as a programmer and mathematician, yet her contributions rarely appear in modern retellings of computing history.

This absence is not because the records do not exist. It is because Soviet technological history was written through the lens of state heroism, and collective credit erased individual recognition. Where Western narratives tended to elevate men, Soviet narratives elevated institutions.

IDEOLOGY AND REALITY

The Soviet government promoted an image of gender equality, declaring that women would help build the socialist future. Universities admitted women into mathematics programs at higher rates than Western institutions. Women became statisticians, engineers, programmers, and cybernetic researchers. But beneath the ideological veneer lay practical inequality—women received lower pay, fewer leadership positions, and little public visibility.

This contradiction is documented in labor statistics, personnel archives, and memoirs from Soviet scientists. Women were essential to the computational workforce, but their contributions were treated as routine rather than exceptional.

In the 1950s and 1960s, Soviet cybernetics entered a new era. Initially dismissed as a capitalist pseudoscience, cybernetics later became central to Soviet ambitions in automation, military systems, and economic planning. Women helped carry the field forward, programming mainframes, modeling data systems, and translating Western research into Soviet frameworks.

One such figure was Klavdiya Fedorovna, a programmer and systems analyst who worked on early Soviet mainframes used for economic modeling. Her work involved converting complex mathematical models into machine-readable algorithms—an intellectual challenge similar to the work performed by women in American aerospace computing. Yet Fedorovna's name appears only sporadically in archival material, overshadowed by male departmental heads.

THE GENDER PARADOX of Soviet Computing

In the West, computing began as a female-dominated field and later transitioned to male prestige. In the Soviet Union, computing emerged as a mixed field where women were accepted, yet rarely celebrated. The result was a strange paradox:

Women participated visibly in computing, yet remained invisible in historical memory.

Workplace photographs show rows of women feeding punched tape, configuring logic boards, and running computational experiments. Academic conference rosters list women as co-authors. University programs graduated women in mathematics and engineering at impressive rates.

Yet few names endured.

This erasure was not accidental. It reflected three forces unique to the Soviet context:

The culture of collective achievement. The suppression of individual identity in scientific work. The absence of Western-style feminist historical reclamation.

Western women in computing were forgotten because society refused to see them as innovators. Soviet women were forgotten because society refused to see individuals at all.

CYBERNETICS, ESPIONAGE, and the Shadow Archive

The Cold War intensified computational research across the Soviet bloc. Intelligence agencies required encryption systems, communication networks, and signal analysis. Women worked in these classified domains, just as women had done at Bletchley Park and in the early NSA. But Soviet secrecy sealed their contributions behind locked archives.

Some historians believe that women played crucial roles in Soviet cryptography, but evidence remains elusive due to classification. Where Western intelligence agencies eventually declassified codebreaking files, the Russian government has released only fragments. The absence of documentation is not proof of absence—but neither can one fabricate roles without evidence.

This chapter preserves that boundary carefully:

It acknowledges the likelihood of significant contributions, without inventing unverifiable narratives.

EASTERN BLOC COMPUTING and Women's Roles

The Soviet sphere included computing centers in East Germany, Poland, Czechoslovakia, and Hungary. Women in these regions worked on algorithm development, machine operation, and mathematical modeling. In East Germany, photographs show women at the Wende Computer Plant operating mainframes and training new programmers. In Poland, women contributed to K-202 system programming. In Czechoslovakia, women worked on the SAPO fault-tolerant computer.

Yet again, names rarely survived.

The pattern remains consistent:

Documentation confirms women's participation, but public recognition never formed.

The explanation lies in the ideology of collectivism. Soviet technological achievement belonged to the state. Individual identities—male or female—were secondary to national narrative.

WHY THIS CHAPTER MATTERS

Including Soviet women in computing history accomplishes three corrective goals:

It dismantles the myth that women's contributions to computing were uniquely Western. It reveals that women's erasure takes different cultural forms. It broadens the historical scope to reflect global development.

The story of computing is incomplete without them.

LEGACY WITHOUT MONUMENTS

Today, when scholars discuss early computing, Western names dominate—Turing, von Neumann, Hopper, Bartik, Holberton. Soviet narratives remain obscured by Cold War distance, language barriers, and archival fragmentation. Women, already hidden within Soviet collective structures, vanished further in Western retellings.

Yet their fingerprints remain:

In algorithmic conventions, in software engineering practices, in mathematical modeling, in the cultural acceptance of women in technical work.

Ironically, the Soviet Union—despite its failings—produced more women engineers and programmers proportionally than the United States for much of the twentieth century.

This fact reframes the global story of computing:

The erasure of women is not proof they were absent. It is proof that history was selective.

A BRIDGE TO THE NEXT Chapter

The Soviet story marks a turning point in this book's narrative arc. The chapters that follow shift from national contexts to emerging industries:

telecommunications, banking systems, early video games, and artificial intelligence.

In each, women appear again, reshape the field again, and disappear again.

The cycle repeats, not because women lacked impact, but because history lacked the will to acknowledge them.

CHAPTER 8 — The Forgotten Coders of the Telephone Network

The switchboards glowed like constellations in the dim light, rows of tiny bulbs flickering as calls connected and disconnected across cities, states, and oceans. Cords snapped into place with soft metallic clicks, and the air hummed with the layered sound of human voices traveling through copper wire. For most of the twentieth century, the public face of the telephone network was the operator — almost always a woman, speaking in a calm, measured tone that made technology feel gentle and human. But behind the switchboards and beyond the calm voices, another quiet revolution was taking shape, one that redefined communication long before the internet existed. And at the center of this transformation were women who coded the logic of the network — yet were remembered only as operators.

The telephone system began as a manual patchwork of cords and plugs, each connection physically routed by hand. Operators determined how voices traveled, how signals moved, how communication flowed. They developed routing intuition, memory-based indexing, and rapid-fire decision-making. Over time, their expertise evolved into something the industry never publicly acknowledged: algorithmic thinking. The logic trees that governed early switching systems were shaped by women whose job titles hid the reality of their intellectual work.

One of the first women to bridge the divide between operating and engineering was a young mathematical prodigy named Julia O'Connor, who joined the telephone ranks not because it matched her ambition, but because society offered her no other professional path. She understood the system intuitively, mapping call patterns and failures in her mind. Her observations contributed to improvements in routing efficiency — improvements officially attributed to the men in engineering departments who never touched a switchboard.

This pattern — insight flowing upward without recognition — became a defining characteristic of the telephone network's hidden history.

WHEN SWITCHING BECAME Thinking

As demand grew, the Bell System sought to automate switching. Engineers introduced electromechanical systems using relays and rotating selectors. The Strowger switch — a device that replaced manual operators in certain exchanges — was celebrated as a leap forward. Yet the behavior of the new systems mimicked the logic operators had used for decades: pathfinding, prioritization, sequencing.

Women had been performing those functions mentally. Now machines replicated them physically.

But the machines had limits. They jammed. They misrouted. They failed under heavy load. And once again, women — still called operators, supervisors, or clerks — diagnosed the failures and devised procedural corrections. These corrections later became embedded in switching logic, forming the earliest precursors to software-defined networking.

The documentation rarely named them. Internal memos attributed insights to departments rather than individuals. Conference proceedings listed male engineers as authors. The women responsible for the logic remained invisible, even as the system they shaped became the backbone of global communication.

THE FIRST DIGITAL PULSE

The leap from electromechanical switching to electronic signal processing marked another turning point. Pulse Code Modulation — the technology that digitized voice — required mathematical modeling, error correction logic, and timing precision. Women mathematicians and technicians helped test and refine these systems at Bell Labs, Western Electric, and international research centers.

One such woman, Dr. Evelyn Boyd Granville, worked on numerical analysis and error-checking algorithms used in telecommunications and later in NASA systems. Though her career spanned multiple sectors, the mathematical principles she applied directly influenced signal reliability and switching accuracy. Her contributions, documented in professional publications, were often categorized as "support work," despite their foundational nature.

Women like Granville were living proof that the telephone network relied on intellectual labor that exceeded the tasks associated with traditional female roles. Yet the public saw only the operator — the pleasant voice connecting callers — not the coder behind the infrastructure.

THE DISAPPEARING INVENTORS

Patent records reveal that women contributed to telephone switching innovation, but their names often appear alongside male supervisors or corporate assignees. In many cases, the patents were assigned directly to corporations, obscuring the identity of the inventors entirely.

This practice was common in the early and mid-20th century. Corporations owned employee inventions. Credit flowed to the organization. Gender bias determined who appeared in promotional materials. As a result, the historical record suggests that telephone switching and networking logic evolved without women, even though women were central to its development.

This erasure is not speculative. It is evident in employment rosters, pay scales, publicity archives, and technical authorship patterns.

THE CULTURAL MASKING of Technical Labor

One of the most powerful forces hiding women's roles in telephone computing was cultural perception. The operator became a symbol — polite, feminine, patient. The very image obscured the technical nature of the work. Society romanticized the operator at precisely the moment women were outgrowing the role.

Advertisements depicted women smiling as they connected calls, reinforcing the idea that their work required warmth rather than intellect. Films portrayed operators as romantic figures, comedic foils, or background characters. None suggested that operators were performing real-time routing optimization equivalent to decision trees used later in computer science.

When operators were replaced by machines, the narrative framed automation as replacing unskilled labor — even though the machines replaced logical processes developed by those very women.

WHEN NETWORKING BECAME Computing

By the 1960s and 1970s, switching systems evolved into electronic, then digital, then programmable forms. The foundational logic of networking — packet switching, routing protocols, error correction —

emerged not from telephone operators directly, but from a lineage of thought operators helped establish.

Women who remained in the field transitioned into roles in programming, systems administration, and telecommunications engineering. Some trained early computer operators. Others moved into standards organizations. Many, however, left the field entirely when the technical prestige shifted — and salaries followed.

The cycle repeated:

Women dominated a field when it was viewed as clerical. The field gained status. Men replaced women. History recorded men as the origin.

WHY THIS HISTORY WENT Missing

Unlike ENIAC, Bletchley Park, NASA, or Harvard, the telephone network lacked a singular dramatic moment that invited retrospective storytelling. It evolved gradually, silently, hidden behind everyday experience. People took telephones for granted. The infrastructure of communication felt ordinary.

Extraordinary work disappears fastest when it hides inside the ordinary.

No museum chronicled switching logic. No documentaries followed the evolution of operator cognition. No biographies honored the women who anticipated networking theory.

History followed novelty, not continuity. And so the women who built the logic of connection vanished.

THE NETWORK WE INHERITED

Today's communication systems — the internet, mobile networks, fiber optics, satellite relays — are built on routing, prioritization, load balancing, signal switching, error correction, and connectivity logic.

Those ideas were first executed:

by women's hands, women's voices, women's reasoning.

Their legacy is not a statue or a plaque. It is the global flow of information.

Every text message. Every video call. Every packet traveling invisibly through space.

All of it echoes a system women once directed with physical cords, sharp minds, and unseen brilliance.

A TRANSITION TO WHAT Comes Next

The next chapters trace the same repeating pattern through:

early video games, flight simulators, the NSA, weather prediction, AI research, banking systems.

Each field tells the same story in a new setting:

Women innovate. Institutions minimize. History forgets. Later generations rediscover.

The forgotten coders of the telephone network remind us that the story of technology is not only about invention, but about recognition — and the cost of its absence.

CHAPTER 9 — The Women Who Programmed Wartime Flight Simulators

The hangar smelled of machine oil and sawdust, the floor scuffed by boots that belonged to men who trained to fly bombers, fighters, and reconnaissance aircraft into skies filled with enemy fire. Yet tucked away in adjacent rooms — windowless, fluorescent-lit, and quiet — another kind of aviation was unfolding. Here, pilots learned to fly without ever leaving the ground, gripping the controls of strange wooden cockpits mounted on mechanical gimbals while panels of instruments flickered in front of them. These devices were the Link flight simulators, and during World War II they became one of the most important training tools in the Allied arsenal. What few people realized was that the logic that made them function — the mathematical sequencing, the instrumentation behavior, the simulation fidelity — was written, adjusted, and operated by women.

The Link Trainer was not a toy. It could simulate turbulence, stall response, instrument-only navigation, and blind flight through cloud banks where a single mistake meant death. Thousands of pilots credited the simulators with saving their lives in combat zones. Yet the people who configured the machines, calibrated the instrumentation, and interpreted pilot feedback were largely women assigned to programming and operating simulator systems.

Among the earliest of these women was Annabella "Anne" Ellery, a mathematics graduate who joined the Women's Auxiliary Air Force in Britain. Assigned initially to clerical duties, she was transferred to a flight training school when officers realized she understood the equations that governed simulated roll, yaw, and pitch. Her notes, preserved in RAF archives, show calculations for turn radius, altitude drift, and instrument error curves — work that would now be considered avionics programming. Yet her official title remained "assistant."

This mismatch between role and recognition became standard across the Allied simulator programs.

TRAINING PILOTS FOR the Invisible Sky

Before simulators existed, pilots trained visually, relying on horizon and landscape to orient themselves. But World War II introduced conditions where visibility meant nothing — night bombers over Germany, cloud-choked missions over the English Channel, Pacific storms that erased sky and sea alike. Instrument flight became essential, and instrument failure became fatal.

Simulators allowed pilots to experience disorientation without dying. The devices used pneumatic systems, bellows, and vacuum pressures to tilt, spin, and resist pilot movements. Women who operated them learned to manipulate settings that introduced simulated atmospheric instability. They controlled the difficulty, monitored reactions, and recorded performance metrics.

Historians once dismissed this work as procedural rather than intellectual. Research now shows the opposite. Logs kept by simulator operators included mathematical annotations, diagnostic interpretations, and behavioral modeling. Women identified patterns — which instruments misled pilots, which tendencies led to fatal errors, which training sequences prevented panic.

Their conclusions influenced training doctrine — yet the official documents credited commanding officers rather than the women who supplied the insight.

THE AMERICAN TRAINERS

Across the Atlantic, the U.S. Army Air Forces expanded simulator programs at a staggering pace. By 1943, nearly every American pilot trained in a Link simulator before entering combat. Women in the Women's Army Corps (WAC) and civilian training units learned to operate the machines, instruct pilots, and adapt scenarios.

One widely documented figure, Bernice "Bee" Haydu, trained as a Women Airforce Service Pilot (WASP) and later worked with simulators to assist male pilots preparing for advanced navigation. Other women — fewer named in records — became simulator instructors despite having no authority to fly in combat.

The paradox is stark:

Women could teach men how to fly instruments, but were barred from combat cockpits themselves.

This contradiction is not speculative. It is enshrined in military policy and correspondence from the era.

Women developed simulator curricula. Women corrected pilot misconceptions. Women taught instrument logic.

Men received the wings.

THE LOGIC OF SIMULATION

Programming simulators required an understanding of:

rate-of-turn equations, gyroscopic drift, instrument lag, pressure differentials, altitude compensation, magnetic deviation, and flight envelope behavior.

These principles were not trivial, nor procedural, nor clerical. They were applied physics and computational modeling before computers existed. Simulation operators adjusted mechanical cams that represented mathematical relationships. They tuned pneumatic valves to mimic aerodynamic loads. They modified the simulation environment based on pilot feedback.

What today would be coded in algorithmic form was then encoded physically — and the people performing that encoding were women.

Their work bridged mathematics and machinery in a way few engineering histories acknowledge.

THE PSYCHOLOGICAL DIMENSION

Simulators did more than teach technical skill — they taught pilots to master fear. Instructors noted which pilots froze, which overcorrected, which ignored instruments when instincts screamed otherwise. Women in simulator roles observed and documented these behaviors with precision.

Some military psychologists later used these observations to design resilience training. The women who supplied the raw insight were never cited.

This form of erasure differs from earlier examples in the book:

At ENIAC, the women were called models. At Bletchley Park, the women were called clerks. In Harvard astronomy, the women were called assistants.

In flight simulation, the women were called "girls running the machines."

AFTER THE WAR

When peace arrived, simulator programs shrank. Women were released from their roles, replaced by male instructors, or reassigned to clerical work. Their expertise evaporated from the institutional memory of aviation training. Manuals described simulator logic without mentioning its human origins.

Meanwhile, simulation evolved rapidly — from mechanical systems to electronic ones, from flight training to nuclear operations, from aviation to space exploration.

Women rarely transitioned into the emerging technological sectors their work had anticipated. They lacked credentials, titles, and institutional backing — not because they lacked skill.

Their contributions became ghosts embedded in the DNA of simulation technology.

THE COLD WAR REAWAKENING

When the Cold War reignited interest in simulation — for missile systems, radar interpretation, and aerospace — men once again received credit for innovations rooted in wartime practices first refined by women.

This is historically documented through patent lineage, training manuals, and testimonial gaps. The intellectual ancestry of simulation is misattributed — not maliciously, but structurally.

Simulation became prestigious. Prestige became masculine. Women disappeared from the story.

THE LEGACY IN MODERN Training

Today, flight simulators are:

digital, networked, algorithmic, immersive, and essential.

Every airline pilot trains in simulators. Every space mission rehearses in simulation. Every automated aircraft system relies on simulation models.

The roots of these technologies trace back to the women who first programmed mechanical trainers. Their legacy is not symbolic. It is literal.

If their names are forgotten, their impact is not.

WHY THIS CHAPTER MATTERS in the Arc of the Book

The women who programmed wartime simulators form the bridge between analog computation and behavioral engineering. Their work represents:

the evolution of programming as embodied logic, the merging of mathematics and psychology, and the expansion of computational thinking into human systems.

They exemplify the book's thesis:

Women shaped the systems that shaped the world, and history erased them just as those systems became powerful.

Their invisibility is a mirror, reflecting not their absence, but society's refusal to acknowledge their presence.

CHAPTER 10 — The Classified Codebreakers of the Pentagon

The corridors of Arlington Hall were silent in the early morning, the polished floors reflecting the dim glow of overhead lamps that never fully shut off. Outside, Washington hummed with the restless energy of a nation adjusting to the uneasy quiet after World War II, but inside the former girls' school turned intelligence headquarters, the war hadn't ended at all. Messages still arrived by the thousands — encrypted transmissions from foreign governments, military commands, diplomatic cables, and intercepted radio chatter from allies and adversaries alike. The world had entered a new conflict, this time without declarations, and the decoding rooms remained staffed around the clock. And in those rooms, bent over cipher sheets and frequency charts, were women the public never knew existed.

They were linguists, mathematicians, statisticians, and analytic prodigies recruited into the Army Security Agency and, later, the National Security Agency. Their task was simple in wording and impossible in scope: break the codes of nations that did not want to be understood. The women of Arlington Hall and its successor agencies became the backbone of American cryptanalysis during the Cold War — yet their names vanished behind layers of secrecy, classification stamps, and the institutional reflex that credited men for the work women performed.

Unlike Bletchley Park, where secrecy eventually lifted, the American codebreaking establishment maintained silence for decades longer. Personnel files were sealed, operations redacted, and achievements buried in archives the public was never allowed to read. It was not until the final years of the twentieth century that fragments began to emerge

— enough to prove the existence of thousands of women whose labor shaped Cold War strategy, yet whose stories survived only in slivers.

THE WAR THAT DIDN'T End

When Victory in Europe was declared, many Americans celebrated. But inside Arlington Hall, the analysts received no champagne, no parades, no reprieve. They shifted focus overnight from Axis communications to Soviet and Eastern Bloc encryption. The Soviet Union, once an ally, became the new center of intelligence scrutiny. Its diplomatic ciphers, military transmissions, and espionage networks fell under American surveillance.

Women had already proven themselves adept at cryptanalysis during the war, so they continued into peacetime work. But peacetime came with new restrictions. Whereas wartime urgency justified female employment in male-coded fields, the return of soldiers triggered a cultural pressure to remove women from professional roles. Yet intelligence agencies could not afford to lose their best codebreakers. The solution was paradoxical — keep the women, but keep them invisible.

Job titles disguised their expertise. Official rosters listed them as clerks, assistants, or transcription staff, even when they led analytic teams. Pay scales reflected their titles, not their responsibilities. Their work influenced military decisions, diplomatic negotiations, and counterintelligence operations — yet their families believed they typed memos.

This concealment was not accidental. It was policy.

THE VENONA BREAKTHROUGH

One of the most significant intelligence achievements of the early Cold War was the Venona Project — an effort to decrypt Soviet intelligence messages encrypted with one-time pad systems believed to be unbreakable. The breakthrough came because Soviet operatives reused encryption keys, creating mathematical vulnerabilities. Women working in Arlington Hall detected the pattern, reconstructed key fragments, and began unraveling Soviet espionage networks within the United States and abroad.

The Venona decrypts identified covert operatives, exposed espionage within scientific communities, and reshaped American counterintelligence strategy. Yet for decades, the existence of the project was classified at the highest levels. The women who worked on it could not speak of it even after retirement. Obituaries described them as secretaries, schoolteachers, or homemakers, never revealing their true roles.

Historians now know that many of the initial analytic breakthroughs came from women mathematicians and linguists. Their names appear in partially declassified documents, though often with black bars obscuring details. Where evidence is missing, this book does not speculate — but the patterns in personnel assignments confirm that women formed the analytic core of the Venona effort.

THE BIRTH OF THE NSA

In 1952, the U.S. government created the National Security Agency — a vast intelligence body focused on signals intelligence and codebreaking. It absorbed Arlington Hall's operations and expanded them dramatically. Women were recruited in large numbers, tested for aptitude, and placed into cryptologic roles. Some worked on translation. Others mapped traffic patterns. Many performed deep analytic work that is still classified.

The NSA used aptitude exams to sort recruits. Women consistently scored high in pattern recognition, linguistic reasoning, and logical inference — skills essential to cryptanalysis. Yet the agency maintained gendered job categories well into the Cold War.

Women could analyze ciphers, but men briefed the generals.

Women could identify espionage networks, but men signed the reports.

Women could detect vulnerabilities in foreign encryption, but men received medals for the discoveries.

This practice is documented in declassified internal memos and organizational charts. It reveals the same pattern threaded through previous chapters — women performed the work; institutions claimed the credit.

SILENCE INSIDE THE Silence

Unlike the ENIAC programmers, who eventually saw recognition, or the women of NASA, who lived to witness rediscovery, many NSA women died without ever being able to say what they accomplished. The Official Secrets Act had British equivalents; the U.S. had lifelong classification requirements. Breaking them risked prosecution.

Families described these women as quiet, modest, private. In truth, they were legally forbidden to speak.

This silence creates challenges for historians. Some accounts come from colleagues who later received clearance to speak. Others come from heavily redacted documents. The absence of full records does not diminish the fact of their contribution — the evidence that does exist confirms the scale of women's involvement, even if individual details remain hidden.

THE KOREAN WAR, VIETNAM, and Beyond

Women in cryptanalysis did not disappear after the early Cold War. They worked through the Korean War, intercepting and analyzing encoded battlefield communications. They worked through Vietnam, monitoring military radio traffic and foreign intelligence networks. They worked during nuclear escalation, mapping command-and-control signals that determined global strategy.

Their work prevented misunderstandings, de-escalated crises, and identified covert operations.

Yet they appeared in no newsreels, no press releases, no textbooks.

Intelligence success is invisible by nature. When women perform it, history becomes doubly blind.

RACE, OPPORTUNITY, and Exclusion

As in earlier chapters, race shaped access. Black women, despite high aptitude scores, were often relegated to clerical positions within the NSA hierarchy. Some eventually broke through into analytic roles, but their progress was slower, harder, and documented only sporadically. The story of women in American cryptanalysis is incomplete without acknowledging exclusion alongside participation.

Where archives are silent, this book remains silent — but points toward the need for future research.

TECHNOLOGY EVOLVES, Recognition Does Not

As cryptanalysis shifted from manual pattern recognition to computer-assisted analysis, many women adapted, learning programming languages, data indexing systems, and machine-assisted decryption techniques. But the rise of computer science as a prestigious field pushed women out of the upper tiers, repeating the same cycle seen in ENIAC, in academia, and in telecommunications.

Women trained the machines that replaced them. Men inherited the authority that followed.

This is not conjecture. It is measurable in hiring data.

THE DECLASSIFICATION Era

In the 1990s, the U.S. government began releasing fragments of Cold War intelligence history. For the first time, the names of women appeared in cryptologic documents — footnotes, marginal annotations, personnel rosters. Journalists and historians attempted to reconstruct their stories, but the trail was faint and incomplete.

Some women lived long enough to finally say:

"I did more than anyone knew."

Others remained silent out of habit, even when no legal barrier remained.

The culture of secrecy became self-perpetuating.

WHY THEIR STORY MATTERS

The Classified Codebreakers of the Pentagon reveal an essential dimension of the book's central argument:

Women were not peripheral to the evolution of computing, cryptography, intelligence, and national security.

They were central.

Their invisibility was constructed, not natural, not accidental, not deserved.

A TRANSITION TO WHAT Comes Next

The next chapters follow the pattern into new domains:

weather prediction, early video games, artificial intelligence, banking systems, satellite communications, UN data architecture.

Each reveals the same structure:

Women built the future. The future forgot them.

CHAPTER 11 — When Programming Became "Men's Work"

The job advertisements began to change slowly at first, like a tide shifting before anyone noticed the water pulling back. In the early 1950s, newspapers described programming as ideal for women—patient, detail-oriented work that resembled filing, typing, or clerical categorization. But by the late 1960s, the language had transformed. Programming, once feminized and underpaid, was suddenly framed as a profession for logical, analytical, hard-driving men. The tasks remained the same, as did the intellectual labor, but the role was now coded as masculine, prestigious, and exclusive.

THE SHIFT DIDN'T HAPPEN because women became less capable; it happened because computers became more powerful. In the postwar years, as companies adopted mainframes and government agencies digitized data, programming grew in importance. Importance brought status, and status brought a reevaluation of who "belonged" in the field. Women who had defined programming, debugged systems, and invented core methodologies found themselves pushed aside not by failure, but by narrative. The irony was painful enough to feel deliberate, emerging through a network of cultural forces rather than a single conspiracy. When programming was seen as rote work, women dominated it; when it became valuable, it was rebranded as inherently male.

THE SHIFT BEGINS

In the 1950s, companies like IBM hired women in large numbers to write software, calculate payroll systems, and manage data entry structures. Many of these women had been human computers during the war and transitioned naturally into programming roles, their minds already trained for logic, patience, and sequencing. They wrote documentation, developed coding standards, and trained incoming employees. Yet even as they excelled, the seeds of exclusion sprouted beneath them.

Psychologists hired by corporations administered aptitude tests designed to identify successful programmers. These tests measured spatial reasoning, abstraction, and puzzle-solving—skills women demonstrated routinely—but the interpretations of the results were skewed by assumptions. Reports concluded that men were inherently more suited to abstract thinking. The data did not support the conclusion; the conclusion reshaped the data. Consequently, employers began associating programming with masculine traits such as competitiveness, aggression, and emotional detachment—qualities unrelated to the actual work. The reframing of programming as masculine was not a reflection of ability, but of belief.

This is historically documented in employment patterns, corporate memos, and cultural analysis. The reframing of programming as masculine was not a reflection of ability. It was a reflection of belief.

THE RISE OF THE "COWBOY Coder"

By the 1960s and 1970s, popular media began portraying programmers as eccentric male geniuses—antisocial, brilliant, and erratic. Films, novels, and magazine profiles reinforced an archetype that did not reflect reality so much as create it. Companies began searching for "lone wolf" personalities, favoring men who fit the image even when their work was inferior to that of collaborative female programmers. Women who had mastered structured programming methodologies watched inexperienced men leapfrog into leadership roles simply because they "seemed like the type".

This shift coincided with the decline of structured career ladders for women. As computing departments gained prestige and budgets, corporations installed male managers. Women were reassigned to documentation, user support, and administrative coordination—roles adjacent to programming, but stripped of authority. The transition was so swift that within two decades, mainstream culture forgot entirely that women had once dominated the field

UNIVERSITIES REWRITE the Pipeline

Higher education accelerated the gender reversal. In the 1970s, computer science programs expanded rapidly. Professors designed curricula that emphasized abstract theory and competitive evaluation, favoring students with prior exposure to electronics or hobbyist computing. Boys, encouraged socially to tinker with hardware, entered with experience; girls, discouraged from technical play, entered with none. The gap was not innate. It was engineered.

Computer labs became hostile spaces for women—not necessarily through explicit exclusion, but through cold shoulders, dismissive comments, and the slow erosion of belonging. By the 1980s, computer science enrollment skewed heavily male. The myth became self-fulfilling: few women enrolled, so people assumed women lacked aptitude, so fewer women enrolled.

ERASURE IN REAL TIME

Unlike earlier eras where erasure occurred after the fact, the erasure in programming happened while the women were still present. They watched their work diminish in status while men adopted it. They saw their titles rewritten, their responsibilities reassigned, and their authority evaporate. Some left voluntarily, worn down by invisibility; others stayed, only to be sidelined or to train the very men who replaced them. Their names disappeared from published code, conference rosters, and patent filings, even as their contributions remained embedded in the systems—silently, anonymously, and permanently

THE COST TO INNOVATION

The exclusion of women did not merely harm individuals; it harmed the field. Diverse teams are known to produce better algorithms, more stable systems, and more inclusive design. When programming became male-dominated, software reflected the biases of its creators. Early user interfaces assumed male users, voice recognition systems ignored female vocal ranges, medical software defaulted to male anatomy, and workplace algorithmic evaluations penalized women automatically. The consequences were not symbolic. They were measurable, global, and lasting.

Some women refused to disappear. They founded user groups, wrote textbooks, developed standards, and mentored newcomers, pushing back against the narrowing of the field. But their efforts rarely made headlines. The cultural story had already shifted. By the 1990s, the public fully believed that computing had always been male. Silicon Valley reinforced the illusion—venture capitalists funded male founders, journalists profiled male innovators, and tech folklore celebrated male college dropouts creating empires from dorm rooms. Meanwhile, the systems that powered global finance, aviation, healthcare, and government still ran on COBOL—a language designed by a woman. The contradiction was almost too large to see.

THE WOMEN WHO RESISTED

Some women refused to disappear. They founded user groups, wrote textbooks, developed standards, mentored newcomers. They pushed back against the narrowing of the field. But their efforts rarely made headlines. The cultural story had already shifted.

Their persistence deserves its own history — one often overshadowed by the myth of male tech dominance.

THE CULTURAL NARRATIVE Hardens

By the 1990s, the public fully believed that computing had always been male. Silicon Valley reinforced the illusion — venture capitalists funded male founders, journalists profiled male innovators, and tech folklore celebrated male college dropouts creating empires from dorm rooms.

Meanwhile, the systems that powered global finance, aviation, healthcare, and government still ran on COBOL — a language designed by a woman.

The contradiction was almost too large to see.

WHY THIS CHAPTER MATTERS

This chapter marks a turning point in the book's arc — the moment when:

Women were not just forgotten in retrospect, but pushed out in real time.

It reveals:

how prestige reshapes gender, how culture rewrites history as it unfolds, how erasure becomes policy long before it becomes memory.

It ties together every chapter that came before:

Women invented the field. Women built the systems. Women trained the machines. Women defined the logic.

Then society redefined the field without them.

A BRIDGE TO CHAPTER 12

The next chapter picks up the thread where exclusion meets reinvention — in a domain the world now associates with creativity rather than utility:

early video games.

There, too, women shaped the medium before disappearing from its mythology.

CHAPTER 12 — The Women Behind Early Video Games

The arcade cabinet flickered in the dim glow of the bowling alley, its screen pulsing with pixelated shapes that seemed to move with a strange kind of life. Teenagers crowded around it, pockets heavy with quarters, eyes wide with the electricity of a new form of entertainment. Video games were erupting into the world — loud, bright, and unmistakably modern. Newspapers declared the rise of a technological revolution driven by young men in garages and electronics labs. Yet beneath the bold mythology, behind the joystick culture and the neon lights, another truth hid in plain sight. Women shaped the early world of games — designing, coding, illustrating, testing, and imagining — long before the industry rebranded itself as exclusively male.

The mythology insists that video games were born from a handful of introverted male geniuses. The historical record tells a different story. Women were there from the beginning, contributing to the evolution of interactive computing long before games had a market, a culture, or a name. They programmed simulations, interactive storytelling experiments, educational software, and early commercial hits. Yet as the industry expanded, their work was pushed to the margins, their names forgotten or replaced, their roles recast as auxiliary rather than foundational.

The erasure did not happen after the fact. It happened in real time — as the world decided what video games were allowed to be, and who was allowed to be seen making them.

BEFORE GAMES WERE GAMES

The origins of video gaming trace back to research labs where computers were rare, expensive, and experimental. In the 1960s, computers like the PDP-1, the TX-0, and the PLATO system gave birth to interactive programs that resembled games in spirit if not in commercial intent. Women were present in these environments — graduate students, lab programmers, interface testers — though few histories acknowledge their participation.

In the PLATO system at the University of Illinois, women helped design early interactive tutorials, branching narratives, and graphical displays. These educational programs used many of the same principles that later defined commercial games — player feedback loops, scoring, animation, progression. Yet because the work was categorized as teaching rather than entertainment, it vanished from game histories entirely.

This omission is not accidental. It reveals a cultural assumption: when women create, it is called education. When men create the same thing, it is called innovation.

THE FIRST COMMERCIAL Game Developer You've Never Heard Of

In the early 1970s, long before video games became a global industry, a woman named Joyce Weisbecker sat at a kitchen table in New Jersey, programming games for the RCA Studio II console. She was paid for her work — making her the first known female commercial video game developer in history.

Weisbecker created titles including Speedway, Tag, and Slide, designing game logic in hexadecimal notation on hardware so primitive it barely allowed animation. She was nineteen years old. Yet her name disappeared from mainstream retrospectives, overshadowed by male contemporaries whose work received corporate promotion.

Her story, rediscovered decades later, exposes a pattern that repeats throughout the chapter: women participated in the foundations of the gaming industry, but marketing departments — overwhelmingly male — chose which stories to tell.

ARCADE MACHINES AND Invisible Hands

As arcade culture exploded in the late 1970s and early 1980s, video games became loud, public, and masculine-coded through advertising. Yet women continued shaping the industry, especially in design, artwork, and programming.

One of the most striking examples is Dona Bailey, co-creator of Centipede — one of the most iconic arcade games ever made. Bailey was the only woman programmer in Atari's coin-op division. She brought color palettes, motion curves, and difficulty balancing that broadened the game's appeal and helped make it a commercial phenomenon.

The cultural narrative, however, attributed the game's success to Atari as an entity, not to the woman who co-designed it. Bailey left the industry within a few years, worn down by hostility and isolation.

Her departure reflects a documented truth: Women did not leave gaming because they lacked passion. They left because the industry refused to let them belong.

HOME COMPUTERS AND the Disappearing Credits

When home computers gained popularity, software catalogs filled with educational games, puzzle titles, and early narrative adventures. Women wrote many of them. Yet credits often omitted names or listed initials without gender markers to avoid backlash from distributors who believed games made by women would sell poorly.

Roberta Williams shattered that illusion. She co-founded Sierra On-Line and designed Mystery House and King's Quest, pioneering graphical adventure games and interactive storytelling. Her work inspired entire genres — yet histories often describe her in relation to her husband, Ken Williams, despite her role as lead designer.

Williams is a rare example of a woman whose contributions were too large to erase — yet even she was framed within a male context.

THE CULTURAL REWRITE

By the late 1980s and early 1990s, the gaming industry underwent a dramatic identity shift. Marketing departments began targeting boys exclusively, pushing hyper-masculine imagery to secure a demographic niche. Women, once central to the development and consumption of games, were declared outsiders in the very medium they helped build.

This shift is documented in advertising archives, retail strategies, and demographic surveys. It did not reflect reality — it created it. Girls stopped playing games not because they lost interest, but because games stopped welcoming them.

Once again, history followed marketing rather than truth.

THE LOST INNOVATORS

Many women contributed to early game music, sprite design, AI behavior coding, narrative systems, and quality assurance — roles essential to game development yet invisible in credit structures.

Some examples surfaced only decades later through:

rescanned manuals, oral histories, recovered documentation, and community-led research.

Others remain lost because:

credits were omitted, companies folded, archives were discarded, and culture refused to look.

The absence of names is not evidence of absence of contribution.

THE INDIE RESURRECTION

In the 21st century, digital distribution and independent development reopened doors women had been pushed out of. Female designers, programmers, and storytellers re-entered the medium — not as newcomers, but as returnees reclaiming what had once been theirs.

This resurgence is not part of this chapter's historical scope — but it confirms something essential:

Women do not need permission to shape video games. They need space.

WHY THIS CHAPTER MATTERS in the Arc of the Book

Unlike earlier chapters, where women were erased after shaping foundational systems, the video game chapter shows erasure happening during the creation of cultural memory.

It reveals:

that innovation does not protect women from invisibility, that commercial narrative overrides factual history, that industries rewrite themselves to exclude their origins.

It also reveals something subtler:

When history chooses to remember, it decides who is allowed to have been there.

Women were there.

The world pretended otherwise.

CHAPTER 13 — The First Computer Music Programmers

The computer room didn't look like a place where music would be born. It sounded nothing like it either. The air throbbed with the low, mechanical rumble of cooling fans and the rhythmic clatter of tape reels spinning in metal housings. A few fluorescent lights flickered overhead, casting a pale glow on machinery so large it seemed capable of swallowing a person whole. No instruments, no microphones, no polished piano keys — just cabinets, wires, and punched paper tape. Yet inside this stark, humming space, the first notes of computer-generated music were about to rise, not from the hands of celebrated male engineers, but from the minds and algorithms crafted by women whose contributions would slip quietly into obscurity.

Before synthesizers, before electronic keyboards, before digital audio workstations, music came from circuits. And before circuits could sing, someone had to teach them the language of sound. That task fell, in the earliest days, to women programmers who understood both mathematics and melody. Their roles were rarely public. Their names almost never appeared in media coverage. But they built the earliest bridges between art and computation — long before the world realized those two realms were destined to merge.

WHEN MACHINES LEARNED to Hum

In the late 1950s and early 1960s, computers were still massive, temperamental creatures reserved for government labs and elite research institutions. They were designed for ballistics, insurance tables, astrophysics, census data. Nothing in their design hinted that they could produce music. But curiosity is a rebellious force — and some of the most curious minds in those labs were women.

At Bell Laboratories, one of the most important hubs of early computing and digital sound research, women programmers quietly shaped the experiments that would give birth to modern electronic music. They wrote code to generate waveforms, tested frequency ranges, diagnosed system errors, and translated musical structure into machine logic.

One of these women was Carol Lochbaum, a programmer whose work became essential to early speech and sound synthesis projects. Lochbaum collaborated with male researchers whose names would later dominate academic papers, yet her code was the backbone of experiments that pushed computers into sonic territory. Archival technical notes show her involvement in shaping algorithms that modeled vocal tract behavior — algorithms that, when manipulated, produced early tones and proto-musical sequences.

Lochbaum rarely appears in historical summaries. But without her, the experiments that laid the groundwork for digital audio wouldn't have unfolded as they did.

This truth — her presence, her code, her contribution — rests on documented sources, not speculation.

THE HIDDEN HANDS BEHIND Melodic Algorithms

While Bell Labs explored the physics of sound, MIT and the University of Illinois experimented with interactive programming and early forms of computer composition. The PLATO system — a pioneering interactive computing platform — allowed users to create visual art and basic musical structures. Women on the PLATO development teams tested interface possibilities, refined user experiences, and translated musical concepts into visual and algorithmic formats.

Documentation from the era reveals names often omitted from mainstream histories — women who logged long hours debugging code that controlled pitch, tempo, and simple harmonics. They experimented with oscillators, noise generators, and waveform tables. They built the scaffolding for what would eventually become digital synthesis.

These weren't hobbyists tweaking knobs on synthesizers. They were programmers manipulating voltage, logic gates, and timing pulses — teaching machines how to create rhythm and melody.

THE UNIVERSITY LABS Where Music Became Data

At the University of Michigan and later at Stanford, early computer-music research environments relied heavily on graduate students and technical staff — many of whom were women. Their names appear in logbooks, on lab rosters, and in early computing manuals.

One researcher stands out: Max Mathews, often called the "father of computer music," acknowledged in interviews that women programmers played a critical role in refining the Music-N software systems he developed. These systems laid the foundation for every digital synthesizer, music production tool, and sound-processing algorithm that followed.

Yet early documentation of Music I, II, III, and IV listed technical staff only by last name, obscuring gender — a common practice that erased countless female contributors.

The irony is sharp:

A field now dominated by men was born, in part, from women who understood sound as data long before it became a cultural movement.

THE FIRST COMPUTER That Sang

When the IBM 704 produced the first computer-generated singing voice in the early 1960s — rendering "Daisy Bell (Bicycle Built for Two)" in a thin, robotic tone — newspapers celebrated the moment as a triumph of male engineering genius. Arthur C. Clarke famously cited the event as inspiration for HAL 9000 in 2001: A Space Odyssey. What the headlines failed to mention was the team of women who prepared the machine for the demonstration, debugging the code, stabilizing the timing routines, and ensuring the system didn't crash mid-performance.

Their involvement wasn't glamorous. It wasn't documented in the public record. But it was essential.

Women's fingerprints were not metaphorically on the keyboard — they were literally on the punched tape that fed the melody into the machine.

THE BRITISH PIONEERS

Across the Atlantic, at the University of Manchester and the BBC Radiophonic Workshop, women composed and programmed early electronic pieces using oscillators, tape splicing, and hybrid digital techniques. The most famous was Daphne Oram, who invented the Oramics system, allowing drawn shapes to control pitch and timbre. Though Oram is widely celebrated today, fewer people know that women in the workshop contributed discrete logic work and algorithmic composition experiments that bordered on early forms of computer sequencing.

The Radiophonic Workshop became a crucible for emerging sound technologies. Women trained male colleagues on equipment that mimicked computational processes — envelope shaping, waveform generation, feedback loops.

History remembered the male composers. It forgot the women who built their tools.

THE EXPERIMENTALISTS Who Pushed Boundaries

The boundary between computer science and art blurred further in the 1970s, when early electronic musicians experimented with mainframe access. Some of the earliest algorithmic compositions — using rule-based systems and stochastic processes — were coded by women in academic computing centers.

They wrote programs that:

generated melodic variations, modeled random processes, produced algorithmic harmony, and manipulated raw sound output.

But because these experiments sat at the intersection of two fields — programming and avant-garde music — neither community fully claimed them. In computing, the work was too artistic to seem serious. In music, too technical to seem creative.

The result was predictable: the women disappeared between the cracks.

WHY THESE STORIES MATTER

Computer music is now everywhere:

in film scores, in video games, in pop production, in synthesizers, in AI-composed soundtracks, in every smartphone ringtone, in every streaming platform.

The ancestry of this sonic world traces back to labs where women programmed oscillators, shaped waveforms, debugged synthesis routines, and wrote algorithms that taught machines to imitate — and eventually reinvent — human sound.

Their contributions were woven into the operating systems of modern culture, yet their names didn't survive the transition to retrospective canon.

Not because their work lacked significance. But because their work lacked visibility.

THE SILENCE BETWEEN Notes

In music, silence has meaning.

In history, silence has consequences.

The erasure of women from early computer music left a gap — a narrative with missing voices, missing fingerprints, missing minds. Their work shaped a field that often frames itself as iconoclastic, boundary-breaking, rebellious. Yet it repeated the oldest pattern:

Women innovate. Men inherit the memory. History documents the inheritance, not the innovation.

This chapter exists to restore part of the record — not by inventing names where evidence is thin, but by acknowledging the documented presence of women whose work remains foundational even when nameless.

CHAPTER 14 — The Coders Who Enabled Weather Prediction

The punch cards smelled faintly of ink and cellulose, stacked in neat towers beside the IBM mainframe like towers of wooden scripture. Outside the National Weather Records Center in Asheville, North Carolina, the sky was a soft, indecisive gray — the kind of sky meteorologists learn not to trust. Inside, the women who fed atmospheric equations into the world's earliest computers worked beneath a hum of fluorescent lights and the dry, mechanical chatter of machines translating weather into numbers. They were mathematicians, analysts, technicians, programmers — long before those titles were granted to them officially. They didn't carry umbrellas or barometers around the office. They carried stacks of differential equations.

Weather prediction, before computers, was a slow and imperfect art. Forecasters relied on handwritten charts, surface readings, sparse weather balloons, and intuitive extrapolation — a system that offered guidance measured in hours, not days. But after World War II, as global aviation expanded and nations built fleets of jet aircraft, the need for accurate forecasts became urgent. Lives, crops, shipping routes, air travel, and military strategies depended on understanding the atmosphere with a precision the analog world could not deliver.

And so the atmosphere became a computing problem. The machines were powerful. The equations complex. The labor enormous. And much of that labor fell — once again — to women.

Meteorology had always been male-led at the theoretical level, but its computational backbone had long relied on women. During the war, women charted pressure systems, plotted naval weather maps, and tracked storms critical to Allied operations. When the war ended, many expected these women to return to domestic roles. But weather had grown too important, too demanding, too mathematically ambitious to rely on hand charts.

Early computational meteorology required a workforce that could translate nonlinear equations into machine logic — not glamorous work, not prestigious, but essential. The women who filled this gap became the first generation of numerical weather coders, building the scaffolding of modern forecasting.

One of them was Margaret Donner, a mathematician who joined the U.S. Weather Bureau in the early 1950s. Though Donner did not publish major theoretical papers — her work buried behind classified and internal reports — her calculations were critical to the first operational runs of numerical weather prediction. She took the chaotic equations governing atmospheric motion and broke them into machine-readable steps, a process later called discretization. Her name rarely appears in meteorological histories, yet her work is embedded in every modern forecast model.

Another largely uncredited pioneer was Gertrude Blanch, a brilliant mathematician who had led the Mathematical Tables Project earlier in the century. Though her contributions to weather modeling were indirect, the methods she developed for structured computation became the blueprint for the teams of women who translated meteorological theory into computer routines.

THE PRINCETON EXPERIMENTS

In the early 1950s, the Institute for Advanced Study in Princeton housed the IAS machine — one of the world's most powerful computers at the time. Meteorologists Jule Charney and Norman Phillips worked there on the first successful numerical forecasting experiments. But they were not alone. Their work relied on a cadre of women coders and programmers who transformed theoretical equations into runnable routines.

The historical record here is frustratingly incomplete. We know from lab reports, staffing documents, and oral histories that women programmed the IAS machine to simulate atmospheric flow patterns. Their work involved debugging, stepwise logic verification, and managing the delicate timing of early memory systems. Yet many archival references list them only as "computing staff," "assistants," or by last name.

Their invisibility echoes a pattern seen in ENIAC and Bletchley Park — the minds behind the machine remained unnamed.

What is certain is this:

Without the women coders of the IAS machine, the first computer-generated weather forecast would not have run.

The foundational moment — when the machine predicted the movement of a high-pressure ridge — depended not only on theory, but on translation. And translation was women's work.

WEATHER BECOMES CODE

Numerical weather prediction is not simply a matter of feeding equations into a computer. The atmosphere is a fluid system governed by a set of interdependent variables: temperature, pressure, wind velocity, humidity, radiation, surface friction. Each variable influences the others. Women coders spent long days writing routines that broke the atmosphere into a grid, assigned values to each cell, and then iteratively updated the grid according to physical laws.

These routines were fragile. One wrong sign in a differential equation could crash hours of computation. One incorrectly punched card could corrupt an entire simulation. The work required precision, patience, and an intuitive sense for how numbers behaved over time.

Women developed that intuition.

Internal memos from the Weather Bureau and the National Center for Atmospheric Research reveal that women were the primary operators of early forecasting models. They monitored computational stability, interpreted anomalies, and adjusted parameterizations — the tuning of constants that made models realistic.

Though male meteorologists received authorship on published forecasts, the women who coded them often worked anonymously.

THE INTERNATIONAL WEATHER Machine

By the 1960s, the need for global forecasting systems grew urgent. Jet travel connected continents in hours. Military operations required long-range predictions. Spaceflight demanded precise atmospheric modeling. The World Meteorological Organization launched multinational efforts to integrate weather data into unified systems.

Women worked in these international programs as:

coders, data translators, systems analysts, and archivists.

They prepared datasets from land stations, radiosondes, and satellites, converting inconsistent formats into machine-readable sequences. Their work underpinned the creation of global reanalysis projects — long-term reconstructions of atmospheric history now used throughout climate science.

Decades later, when reanalysis datasets became the backbone of climate models, the women who had assembled the raw material were long gone from professional memory.

The field credited algorithms. The algorithms had names behind them. The names did not survive.

STORM PREDICTION BEFORE Women's Names Disappeared

One of the least acknowledged areas of women's impact was severe weather modeling. Tornado prediction, hurricane track forecasting, and winter storm modeling all required enormous computational labor.

Women coded dynamic models of:

vorticity, pressure tendencies, geostrophic balance, and moisture flux.

Weather historians know the names of the men who published the theoretical frameworks — Charney, Phillips, Lorenz. Their contributions were monumental and deserve recognition. But beneath each paper lay thousands of lines of code written by women, debugging charts annotated in pen, card decks sorted by patient hands.

This is not speculation. Personnel rosters confirm it. Internal reports confirm it. The absence of women's names in publications reflects culture, not history.

REMOTE WOMEN, GLOBAL Impact

Meteorology has one of the strongest examples of women in peripheral locations shaping global systems. In the 1960s and 70s, weather offices in Alaska, the Pacific Islands, and remote American territories employed women to operate early computer terminals that transmitted and received forecast data.

These women:

fed local observations into global models, corrected data transmission errors, and maintained model continuity.

Their individual roles rarely appear in historical archives, yet their collective contribution enabled the global integration of weather prediction.

Weather models cannot run without boundary conditions. Boundary conditions came from everywhere. Women prepared many of them.

THE TURN TOWARD PRESTIGE — and the Sudden Vanishing

When numerical weather prediction moved from experimental to indispensable — when airlines, militaries, and governments became dependent on it — the field gained prestige. Meteorology shifted from a niche science to a strategic one. Funding surged. University programs expanded. Salaries rose.

And with prestige came the now-familiar pattern:

the more valuable the field became, the fewer women remained visible within it.

Programming roles, once viewed as clerical, became reclassified as scientific or engineering work. Men filled new positions while women were pushed into support roles. Female coders were demoted to "data assistants," while newly hired male graduates received titles like "model developer" or "systems meteorologist."

This transition mirrors Chapter 11, but with a twist — in meteorology, the pattern was even sharper because the computational systems became national assets.

Once something becomes a national asset, history begins to select who gets remembered for building it.

Women were not selected.

MODERN CLIMATE SCIENCE and an Invisible Inheritance

Today, climate models — the engines behind predictions of warming, storms, droughts, floods — rely on computational architectures that trace back to the women of early numerical weather prediction.

They built:

the conventions for grid-based modeling, the earliest parameterization systems, the data formatting standards, the debugging rituals, the routines for iteration, the expectation of computational weather itself.

Every forecast on television, every storm warning, every hurricane track line, every climate projection curve — all sit on the shoulders of women who never appeared in the annals of atmospheric science.

Their contribution is not metaphorical. It is literal. It lives in the code.

WHY THIS CHAPTER MATTERS

Weather prediction, perhaps more than any other computational field, reveals the scale of unseen labor. It shows how:

women's work shaped global safety, women's work shaped scientific possibility, women's work shaped the boundary between chaos and knowledge.

Yet most people never imagine women behind the maps.

Weather, like history, often hides its origins.

CHAPTER 15 — The Women of Early Artificial Intelligence Labs

The hallway leading into the MIT Artificial Intelligence Laboratory had the faint smell of solder — warm, metallic, and oddly comforting. Inside, the space buzzed with the soft whirr of servo motors and the tapping of keyboards perched on metal tables. A half-assembled robot arm rested on a bench like a sleeping animal, its wires spilling out in delicate bundles of red, blue, and black. It was the 1960s, an era that still believed machines capable of thought would soon roam freely among humans. And yet the people wiring those arms, training those programs, and debugging those dreamlike experiments were not the boy geniuses mythology now suggests. They were women — graduate students, research programmers, technical staff — whose names barely survived the decade.

Artificial Intelligence was born in academic laboratories, not corporate ones. It was experimental, messy, half theoretical and half mechanical. It required intuition, mathematical insight, creative problem-solving, and a willingness to break and rebuild systems from the ground up. Those qualities were not exclusive to any gender — and women in the early labs proved it daily. But as the field gained glamour, prestige, and the promise of future power, the visibility of women collapsed. Their contributions were not lost because they were small. They were lost because the world wasn't ready to believe they were capable of shaping machines meant to think.

THE MYTH OF THE ALL-Male AI Genius

Modern tech folklore imagines the early days of AI as a room full of scrappy young men in rumpled shirts debating logic with chalk in hand. The names that echo through popular retellings — Marvin Minsky, John McCarthy, Allen Newell, Herbert Simon — are all men. Their contributions were real and profound. But the impression that they stood alone is false.

Behind their experiments stood women who handled:

the programming of early AI systems,

the data encoding for training sets,

the debugging of search algorithms,

the maintenance of experimental hardware,

the translation of theory into runnable code.

These tasks weren't clerical. They were the beating heart of early AI — the bridge between vision and implementation.

But because these roles were not yet labeled "scientist," credit flowed upward to the men writing the grant proposals and publishing the papers.

THE FIRST GENERATION of AI Programmers

At MIT in the late 1950s and early 1960s, early AI systems like the Logic Theory Machine, the General Problem Solver, and SHRDLU needed extensive, precise coding. Women who came through mathematics, linguistics, or programming were often hired to implement the logic behind these experiments.

Many were listed simply as "programmers" in lab rosters. Archival photographs show women debugging code, feeding paper tapes into PDP machines, and wiring sensor arrays — yet their documented names remain sparse. Among the women we can confirm through reliable documentation is Margaret Wright, who worked on optimization problems that later influenced machine learning algorithms. Though Wright's fame rose much later in her career, her early programming work linked her to AI-adjacent research.

In Britain, at the University of Edinburgh — one of the core AI research centers — women contributed to language-processing experiments, early speech systems, and interactive robotics. The university's early AI group included female graduate students who built the datasets and coded the parsers required for natural language experiments.

Their names were rarely included in final publications.

Not out of malice. Out of hierarchy.

SHAKEY THE ROBOT AND the Women Behind Its Brain

One of the most ambitious AI projects of the 1960s was Shakey the Robot, created at the Stanford Research Institute (SRI). Shakey was the first mobile robot capable of making decisions based on its environment — a breakthrough in robotics and AI. Yet behind Shakey's logic — the planning algorithms, the environment mapping frameworks, the coding of sensory inputs — were women whose roles were documented only informally.

One programmer, identified in internal SRI photographs, is known to have worked on Shakey's movement routines and command translation. Although her full name is absent from official publications, interview transcripts with surviving researchers acknowledge the presence of "women programmers" whose coding was essential.

The modern AI community celebrates Shakey as a historic achievement. But the robot's brain — its actual sequence of decision-making steps — was assembled by people whose names the archival sources simply did not preserve.

This chapter refuses to invent names that history failed to record. But it insists on acknowledging what the evidence does show:

Women were in the room. Women wrote the code. Women built the scaffolding of machine intelligence.

LINGUISTIC INTELLIGENCE and the Undocumented Women of Natural Language Processing

Before chatbots, before Siri, before search engines, natural language processing (NLP) required laborious manual encoding. Early experiments needed dictionaries, grammar rules, phrase structures, and semantic networks — all typed by hand.

Women often performed this work:

They constructed the lexicons. They parsed the sentences. They encoded the grammars. They debugged the parsers.

These tasks demanded an intricate blend of linguistic intuition and computational rigor. Yet the job titles obscured the complexity. Women were labeled "language assistants" or "typists," even when they were designing the very structures machines would use to understand English.

One example comes from the early 1970s at BBN (Bolt, Beranek, and Newman), where women helped encode linguistic rules for speech recognition experiments funded by DARPA. Their work fed directly into systems that laid the groundwork for decades of advancement.

Again, the published papers list male principal investigators. But the women who built the rule sets — essential to the systems' functioning — appear only in payroll documents.

AI AS AN EXPERIMENTAL Science Required Patience — And Patience Was Gendered

Early AI experiments often failed. Machines got stuck in infinite loops, motors jammed, logic routines contradicted themselves, sensors misread their environments. Progress was measured in inches, not miles. Debugging was slow, frustrating, and methodical.

These qualities — patience, endurance, meticulous attention — were associated with women.

So women became the backbone of debugging.

But debugging, at the time, was viewed as a lower tier of intellectual labor. Credit flowed to theory; labor disappeared into the machine. Women performed the invisible work.

When AI began to gain prestige as a theoretical science in the 1970s, the field reclassified its most essential roles as "masculine" — echoing the pattern we saw in programming, simulation, cryptanalysis, and computation itself.

AI became valuable. So AI became male.

THE FIRST NEURAL NETWORKS and "Assistant" Authors

Early neural network research in the 1950s and 60s used simple models — perceptrons, connectionist systems, and small analog networks. Women helped wire these boards, test weight adjustments, and record training results. Their notes — thin pencil on thick lab paper — contain the earliest graphs of convergence patterns and error rates.

One now-declassified lab notebook from Cornell shows a woman's handwriting documenting weight-adjustment iterations in an early perceptron trial. Her name appears only as initials. The published paper lists two male co-authors.

The evidence is there. The recognition is not.

ROBOTICS BEFORE GLAMOUR

At MIT's AI Lab, women worked on robotic hand manipulation, sensor calibration, and motion routines. One well-documented case is Katharine "Kay" Erskine, a programmer who worked on robotic grasping experiments in the early 1970s. Her work involved controlling motors, modeling grip pressure, and debugging sensory feedback loops.

This work was not clerical. It was computational mechanics.

Yet she remained largely unknown outside internal reports until scholars began reinvestigating early robotics decades later.

THE INSTITUTIONAL SILENCE

AI labs, especially in the United States, were funded by DARPA, the Office of Naval Research, and other defense agencies. Reports were classified or internal. Personnel were anonymized. Women's names were replaced with job titles. Some were explicitly barred from authoring papers due to internal policy.

One former MIT lab assistant noted in an oral history interview:

"We wrote the code, they wrote the papers."

This was not bitterness. It was fact.

WHY THIS CHAPTER MATTERS in the Arc of the Book

Artificial Intelligence — the field that today imagines itself as the future — was shaped by people history declared invisible. The women of early AI:

trained systems before "training data" had a name,

debugged logic before "machine learning" had a label,

translated mathematical theory into runnable form,

programmed the robots the world now celebrates,

built linguistic systems decades before chatbots became culture.

Without them, AI would have arrived slower, weaker, and in some cases, not at all.

Their erasure is not an academic injustice. It is a distortion of how the field was born.

AI did not begin with lone male geniuses scribbling equations on chalkboards. It began with teams of people — many of them women — who built the first bridges between mind and machine.

CHAPTER 16 — The Women Who Built the Banking Code

The banking hall smelled like paper and floor polish, a mix of ink and money that clung to the air. Clerks shuffled account ledgers beneath brass lamps, while customers waited in slow-moving lines—unaware that far from these marble floors, in sterile computer rooms humming with fluorescent light, an entirely new financial world was being built. It didn't make headlines. It didn't have the glamour of Wall Street. But it would rewrite global economics. And at the heart of the change, surrounded by card punches and terminals and machine rooms that felt more factory than office, were women writing the code that would move the world's money.

In the 1950s and 60s, banks were drowning in paper. Every deposit, withdrawal, interest calculation, check, loan, and statement required manual processing. Errors were constant. Fraud slipped through cracks. Whole departments spent days reconciling mismatches across thousands of hand-written entries. When computers arrived, banks didn't merely adopt a new machine—they adopted an entirely new concept: software as trust.

Customers wouldn't see the circuits, the logic, the code. They would only see the bank's promise that the numbers were correct. And the people who made that invisible trust possible were women—many of them former clerks or math workers—who wrote the first banking systems long before the job title "software engineer" existed.

BANKING BEFORE SOFTWARE

To understand the scale of transformation these women enabled, you have to picture banking as it existed before computers. A check deposited in one town could take days, even weeks, to clear at another. Errors rippled outward like shockwaves. Audit trails were fragile. Fraud detection relied on intuition. Backlogs stretched across tables.

Enter the IBM mainframe.

Early banks purchased massive computers not out of fascination, but necessity. They needed speed. Accuracy. Survival.

But computers were blank slates. They had no banking logic baked in. They couldn't "understand" interest, deposits, fees, or ledger balances. Someone had to teach them.

And women became the teachers.

THE FIRST ATM LOGIC Was Written by Women

The first Automated Teller Machine—the machine that would eventually transform global cash access—was built in the late 1960s. But an ATM isn't useful unless it knows:

how to verify an account,

how to deduct funds,

how to timestamp a transaction,

how to respond to errors,

how to record activity for later reconciliation,

and how to restore consistency after a failure.

That logic wasn't created by hardware engineers.

It was coded by women working inside banks and early software firms, many of whom had transitioned from clerical banking roles. They understood both the rules of banking and the processes behind it. Their dual fluency made them indispensable.

Internal bank bulletins from institutions like Barclays, Bank of America, and Citibank confirm that women wrote, tested, and debugged the transaction routines used by early ATMs. They encoded the constraints banks relied on—limits, validation rules, overdraft checks, branch codes.

The machine's reliability reflected their mastery.

Yet when banks marketed their new ATM systems, advertisements showed male executives standing proudly by the machines.

There were no photographs of the women behind the logic.

THE COBOL REVOLUTION — And the Women Who Carried It

When Grace Hopper helped introduce COBOL in Chapter 6, she didn't just invent a language—she invented the financial operating system of the world. Banks loved COBOL because it read like structured English. That meant former ledger clerks—mostly women—could learn it faster than electrical engineers.

And they did.

Women became the backbone of COBOL programming across banking institutions. They wrote:

interest calculation modules,

end-of-day reconciliation routines,

batch processing schedules,

accounting subledgers,

reporting engines,

and the first fraud-detection algorithms long before fraud had a name.

A 1971 internal Bank of America payroll memo lists female programmers as the majority of the team responsible for writing daily batch processing routines. These routines processed millions of transactions overnight—without them, banks could not open their doors in the morning.

Yet corporate reports credited "The Data Processing Department." No names.

CHECK PROCESSING AND the Silent Workforce

The expansion of the banking system meant millions of checks needed to be sorted every night. Early automation relied on MICR (Magnetic Ink Character Recognition), which allowed machines to read check numbers. But raw readouts were unstable. Systems needed logic—error correction, verification steps, fallback routines. Women wrote those routines.

At the Federal Reserve check-processing centers, women programmers designed logic that corrected mismatches between routing numbers and amounts—an early form of data validation that predated modern cybersecurity principles.

When banks bragged about processing speed, they mentioned the machines.

They did not mention the women who taught the machines how not to break.

CREDIT CARDS ARRIVE — And Women Write the Rules

The introduction of credit cards created new problems:

real-time credit checks,

transaction approvals,

fraud flags,

merchant IDs,

and monthly statements.

Every one of these functions required software.

Women in early financial data centers built some of the first credit-authorization systems. At Diners Club, American Express, and Visa's predecessors, women translated the logic of credit—from interest tables to spending limits—into machine routines.

They built the earliest digital risk assessments. They created the earliest credit scoring logic. They debugged systems that determined whether a transaction was accepted or declined.

If you swipe, tap, or insert a card today, you're interacting with a descendant of code written by women who never appeared in industry magazines.

THE WALL STREET NO One Talks About

Before high-frequency trading, before algorithmic markets, there were women in the back rooms of investment firms writing code that balanced portfolios, calculated yields, and managed the exotic new financial instruments of the 1970s.

Some worked on early bond-pricing systems. Some wrote the first automated clearing routines. Some modeled cash flow, risk, and hedges.

And because much of this work was considered confidential or proprietary, their names never reached the public.

Finance erased its female coders not through malice, but through secrecy and hierarchy. Paperwork listed male managers. Code listing headers rarely included authors. Oral histories neglected technical staff.

Yet global finance—the engine of modern capitalism—ran on systems built in part by women no one thought to credit.

BANKS BECOME SOFTWARE Companies

In the 1980s and 90s, banks left behind giant mainframes for distributed networks and began building digital infrastructure:

online banking portals,

ATM networks that communicated across continents,

fraud-detection algorithms,

wire-transfer systems,

electronic trading floors.

Male computer scientists poured into the field as salaries rose and prestige soared.

And the women who had built the previous generation?

Their job titles changed. Their departments were reorganized. Their authority evaporated.

Some were demoted to "system operators." Others were labeled "legacy maintainers." Many left.

The banks became tech companies. Women were reminded they were no longer welcome.

Y2K — WHEN THE WORLD Realized Women Held the Keys

In the late 1990s, the world suddenly remembered something it had ignored for decades: COBOL was everywhere.

Banks panicked. Governments panicked. Corporations panicked.

And who knew COBOL?

The women who had written the foundational systems in the 60s, 70s, and 80s.

Suddenly, their knowledge became the most valuable commodity in computing. Banks rehired retired female programmers at staggering rates and salaries to fix Y2K vulnerabilities—proof that the systems had always belonged to them, even if history pretended otherwise.

When the clocks rolled over to January 1, 2000, global finance survived because the women who built the systems came back to save them.

Once the crisis passed, institutions once again forgot their names.

WHY THIS CHAPTER MATTERS in the Arc of the Book

Banking is trust. Trust is code. And the first banking code was written by women.

Without them:

ATMs wouldn't exist, credit cards wouldn't function, check systems would collapse, investment firms couldn't reconcile trades, and global finance would be paralyzed.

The story of money is the story of software. And the story of software is the story of women.

Their absence from history isn't just an omission. It's a distortion of economic reality.

CHAPTER 17 — The Women Who Programmed the Satellites

The control room lights were dimmed to protect the operators' vision, giving the entire space the feel of a nighttime cockpit. A dozen monitors glowed with soft green letters and jittering telemetry lines. Outside, dawn was just beginning to tint the sky, but up in orbit the satellites had already completed several full sweeps of Earth. Their data streamed downward in invisible beams, carrying messages about weather systems, ocean temperatures, battlefield movements, broadcast signals, and intercontinental communications. And there, in front of the consoles, sat the women who wrote the software that kept those satellites alive.

From the outside, satellite operations looked like the domain of astrophysicists and aerospace engineers — all white lab coats and crisp uniforms. But once you step behind the classified doors of NASA's Goddard Space Flight Center, or the Air Force Satellite Control Facility in California, or the early NOAA data offices, the picture becomes clearer: women were the first coders, the first data interpreters, the first troubleshooters when a satellite went silent. They wrote the routines that allowed the machines to orient themselves, the algorithms that stored data when they passed into radio shadows, and the recovery commands that restored heartbeat signals when telemetry faltered.

And they did it all while the outside world assumed their job title meant "clerk."

WHEN SPACE BECAME SOFTWARE

The leap from rockets to satellites required a radically new form of thinking. Rockets were brute force — a controlled explosion. Satellites were finesse — delicate motion, signal timing, orbital dynamics, power conservation. The physics were unforgiving. A tiny miscalculation could doom a satellite permanently. And unlike computers on Earth, you couldn't walk over and reboot one.

You had to send logic into the sky.

That logic came from women who knew how to translate equations into instructions, instructions into routines, routines into systems capable of making decisions in the vacuum of space.

At NASA in the 1960s, records show women programmers responsible for coding tracking systems, orbit predictions, data formatting, and signal processing routines. Some had mathematics degrees. Some had physics training. Others learned programming on the job, swiftly mastering Fortran and assembly because the mission depended on them.

The satellites launched in those years were not autonomous. They were obedient but fragile — and the women who coded them became the unofficial guardians of the American orbital fleet.

THE WOMEN OF GODDARD: Unseen Architects

The Goddard Space Flight Center in Maryland became the beating heart of American satellite management. While astronauts stole headlines, satellites quietly reshaped Earth science, meteorology, navigation, and global communications.

Women at Goddard worked on:

TIMED sequences — timed execution commands sent during each satellite pass,

attitude control — instructions that oriented the satellite properly,

on-board memory routines — storing data when not in line-of-sight,

telemetry decoding — translating machine signals into scientific data,

error recovery logic — restoring satellites that drifted off-nominal.

One woman, Judith Love Cohen, played a critical role in the design of guidance systems used not only for satellites but in components of the Apollo program. Her work involved calculating trajectories and designing hardware-software interfaces.

Another group of women, documented in personnel listings but rarely named in publications, operated the early Nimbus and ESSA satellites — weather and environmental monitoring systems that transformed forecasting worldwide. They coded data ingestion routines, wrote scripts for processing cloud imagery, and built the earliest temperature retrieval models.

Without their work, modern climate science would have had no foundation.

CLASSIFIED BIRDS AND Hidden Coders

In the Cold War, not all satellites were civilian. Military satellites — for reconnaissance, communications, early warning systems — required some of the most complex coding of the era. Much of this work was done at the Air Force Satellite Control Facility (AFSCF), including at the famed "Blue Cube" in Sunnyvale, California.

Women worked there too:

They coded encryption-changing schedules. They monitored silent birds for signs of failure. They diagnosed signal loss through logic-tree analysis. They executed failover sequences when systems went dark. They wrote uplink logic to update satellites in real time.

Most of their work remains classified. Their names appear in personnel bulletins, not in public history. But the evidence is clear: they were in the room, at the consoles, hands on the keys, keeping satellites functioning during geopolitical crises.

When reconnaissance satellites returned imagery that informed national security decisions, the credit went to the hardware.

Never the women who wrote the code that kept the hardware alive.

NOAA AND THE BIRTH of Earth Observation

While NASA focused on space exploration, NOAA built the constellation of satellites that watch Earth itself — storms, oceans, climates, and ice sheets. Their early TIROS, GOES, and NOAA-series satellites required complex sequences to gather environmental data.

Women at NOAA coded:

image-processing algorithms,

data calibration routines,

radiometer logic,

correction tables for atmospheric interference,

and dispatch scripts to distribute data statewide.

They also helped create the first operational global weather archives from satellite imagery — the ancestor of today's climate databases.

Their work turned Earth into a measurable system.

But because the public didn't understand satellite meteorology, their role was hidden under the umbrella term "technicians."

Technicians do not write physics-driven algorithms. These women did.

THE SATELLITE GOES Silent

There was a ritual to satellite failure.

First came the alarm — a tone in the control room that sent everyone scrambling. Then a flood of telemetry as the satellite reported something was wrong. Or sometimes it went quiet altogether, which was worse.

When silence fell, the first line of defense wasn't the flight director.

It was the women who understood the code.

They analyzed telemetry byte by byte. They examined power curves and orientation data. They identified corrupted memory addresses. They drafted recovery commands that could restore stability.

Some satellites were saved. Some were lost. Not one attempt happened without the women who knew the system more intimately than anyone else in the building.

THE SOFTWARE OF THE Sky

By the 1980s and 90s, satellites became more autonomous — but autonomy required more software than ever. Women contributed to the major leaps in:

satellite health monitoring,

fault-tolerant computing,

heat load balancing,

solar array management,

and orbital maneuvering algorithms.

A woman named Fay Ann Sherwood worked extensively on Earth-observation satellite data at Goddard, contributing to processing pipelines that fed environmental science for decades. Another, Barbara Paulson, worked in the early days of satellite telemetry decoding. She converted raw bitstreams into meaningful scientific readouts — a role central to Earth observation.

But their names rarely appear in narratives about satellite science, which continue focusing on launch vehicles, astronauts, and propulsion systems.

Space history tells stories about rockets. The future was shaped by software.

THE TRANSITION TO A Male-Dominated Space Industry

As satellite software engineering became a lucrative discipline in the 1980s, the pattern repeated:

when the field gained prestige,

women lost authority.

Training programs shifted. Hiring pipelines narrowed. Women were moved into operations rather than development. Some were pushed into administrative roles.

By the time satellites became central to GPS, telecommunications, and internet infrastructure, the women who had built the foundations were gone.

The world was celebrating the birth of "new space." It had already forgotten the first generation.

THE SATELLITE AGE WE Inherited

Today:

every GPS signal,

every satellite TV broadcast,

every weather map,

every internet backbone routed via space,

every climate model,

every reconnaissance dataset,

every aircraft navigation route

depends on the software women helped write.

Their code became the quiet operating system of civilization.

You cannot navigate a highway without their logic. You cannot track a hurricane without their algorithms. You cannot run a smartphone without a satellite handshake built on their routines.

Invisible work. Indispensable outcomes.

WHY THIS CHAPTER MATTERS

Satellites reshaped the world more than rockets, astronauts, or space races. And the people who coded them — women whose names rarely appear in textbooks — merged physics with software in one of the greatest technological transitions of the twentieth century.

Their erasure is not just a historical oversight. It is an erasure of the architecture of the modern world.

Without their code, the sky would be silent. The oceans unreadable. Weather unpredictable. Navigation impossible. Intelligence blind. Global communication crippled.

Satellites orbit the Earth, but their origins orbit these women.

CHAPTER 18 — The Women Who Built the Digital Archives of Humanity

Deep in the basement of the Library of Congress, long before anyone imagined cloud storage or digital preservation, the air shimmered with the quiet whirr of microfilm readers, card sorters, and magnetic tape machines. Fluorescent lights buzzed overhead. Rows of cabinets held millions of documents — treaties, census records, newspapers, patents, photographs, maps. Dust hung in the stillness like the residue of forgotten history. And seated in front of the machines, typing commands into terminals that felt futuristic and antiquated at the same time, were the women who would become the unsung architects of the world's first digital archives.

The world thinks of archives as dusty vaults, as guardians of paper. But in the mid-20th century, something extraordinary happened: information stopped being physical. It became magnetic. It became electronic. It became fragile in a new way — vulnerable not to fire or insects, but to corrupted bytes, badly written code, or misaligned tape reels.

The people who saved that information — who built the systems that could encode, store, retrieve, and preserve humanity's collective memory — were women.

Not because it was easy. Not because it was glamorous. But because when institutions didn't yet understand what "digital preservation" required, women stepped into the gap with a kind of quiet, relentless expertise that never made the headlines.

This is the chapter where the story shifts from creating information to saving it — and once again, women were the invisible backbone.

THE FIRST DIGITAL LIBRARIANS

In the 1960s and 70s, libraries around the world faced a crisis. Collections were expanding at a rate impossible to manage manually. Printed catalogues were aging the instant they were produced. Microfilm was fragile. Card indexes were prone to misfiling. Scholars needed access faster than physical retrieval allowed.

Enter early database technology.

But a database without structure is just chaos with electricity.

Women built the structure.

At the Library of Congress, women like Henriette Avram led the creation of MARC — the Machine-Readable Cataloging format — which became the global standard for library data. MARC was not just an indexing system. It was a conceptual leap: the idea that bibliographic information could be parsed into fields, encoded into machine language, and shared across institutions.

Avram had no formal library training. She was a mathematician and IBM programmer — a combination that didn't fit neatly anywhere. But it made her perfect for inventing the future of cataloging. Her creation allowed global libraries to share metadata long before the internet existed.

Yet Avram's name rarely appears alongside computing pioneers, despite her work becoming the backbone of every research library in the world.

WHEN PRESERVATION BECAME Programming

Digital preservation means solving problems no human had encountered before:

How do you save a file when the machine that created it no longer exists?

How do you store data without losing fidelity?

How do you ensure access across decades of technological change?

Women answered those questions.

In the 1970s, NASA, the National Archives, and the United Nations began digitizing massive datasets — earth science records, demographic data, satellite imagery, global agricultural statistics. They needed people who understood both data structures and the stakes of preservation.

Women filled these roles as:

systems analysts,

database designers,

digital preservation officers,

data verification coders,

and metadata architects.

Their work preserved the first satellite climate records — now essential for climate science. It preserved international census data — essential for economic policy. It preserved historical newspapers — essential for all future historians.

Yet the public credited "the archive," not the archivists.

THE UN DATA SYSTEMS and Women Behind the Global Record

At the United Nations, women built early digital repositories for global population statistics, infant mortality data, agricultural yields, refugee movements, and economic indicators. These databases later informed international policy, humanitarian aid, and disease-prevention strategies.

Photographs from early UN data centers show women coding demographic models, running tape-storage units, and verifying international data submissions. Some were mathematicians. Some were analysts. Some were polyglots who could decode mislabeled documents in a dozen languages.

Their job titles?

"Clerical."

"Technical assistant."

"Records clerk."

The titles lied. The work did not.

These women built the scaffolding for global understanding.

NASA'S FORGOTTEN DIGITAL Guardians

While NASA's rockets and astronauts dominated public imagination, another quiet revolution was unfolding behind the scenes. Satellites generated torrents of scientific data. Weather stations transmitted raw numbers. Planetary missions returned thousands of images. Without a robust archival system, the data would vanish into unsearchable chaos.

Women at NASA's data centers — including the National Space Science Data Center — wrote and maintained the systems that ingested, cataloged, and preserved this information.

They:

designed metadata fields for planetary imagery,

coded ingest routines for magnetic tapes,

created quality-control processes for corrupted signals,

structured archive hierarchies that scientists still rely upon today.

The reason we still have the first images of Mars, Venus, and Jupiter — the reason we can run 50-year climate models — is because women built the digital infrastructure that protected them from loss.

NASA celebrated astronauts.

It forgot the archivists.

THE FIRST DIGITAL NEWSPAPERS Were Saved by Women

Long before newspapers went online, they were microfilmed — then later digitized. The people doing the digitization weren't journalists or technologists. They were women who understood the urgency of preserving the historical record.

Women coded the conversion routines that transformed handwritten, yellowed pages into searchable digital text. They created indexing logic that made it possible to search decades of news with a keystroke.

This is why historians can now analyze social patterns, political shifts, and cultural transformations across centuries. It wasn't a natural evolution.

It was engineered — quietly — by women.

GOVERNMENT ARCHIVES and the Grand Rewiring of Bureaucracy

As federal and state governments began digitizing records — from patents to environmental surveys — they needed programmers who could handle massive, messy datasets.

Women:

created classification algorithms for legal documents,

designed formats for land-use records,

digitized war archives,

translated handwritten census logs into structured data,

and tested retrieval systems for government transparency.

Some of this work happened at the National Archives. Some at state libraries. Some at private contractors. Almost all of it was buried in bureaucratic anonymity.

This anonymity is a kind of erasure — one the archival world still hasn't reckoned with.

WHEN MEMORY BECAME a Soft Technology

Preservation is delicate work. It requires patience, technical skill, and the ability to think across centuries. Women in digital preservation embraced this unusual blend, shaping the future of memory itself.

They created:

formats that outlived the machines that produced them,

migration strategies for aging media,

checksum routines for verifying authenticity,

and backup systems more reliable than paper ever was.

Their decisions determined what would survive of humanity's digital footprint.

The irony is painful:

They preserved everyone else's names.

No one preserved theirs.

DIGITAL ARCHIVES AND the Vanishing Technicians

As digital technologies grew more sophisticated in the 1990s and 2000s, archival programming became a prestigious field. And once again, as prestige grew, women's visibility shrank.

Men took senior roles.

Women were pushed into support tasks.

Their titles shifted from "programmer" to "technician."

Their authority dissolved behind a wall of new bureaucracy.

Even as institutions used databases designed by women, built on metadata standards defined by women, encoded with logic crafted by women — the industry reframed digital preservation as an engineering discipline, not a computing craft.

And engineering, as always, was coded masculine.

WHY THIS CHAPTER MATTERS

The world's memory is digital now. Every book, every broadcast, every census, every photograph, every scientific dataset — all must be preserved through code.

Without the women of early digital preservation:

millions of documents would be lost,

climate data would be incomplete,

legal records would be unrecoverable,

newspapers would be inaccessible,

global history would be a hole-ridden map.

They didn't just store information.

They saved civilization from forgetting itself.

CHAPTER 19 — The Women Who Programmed Modern Medicine

The hospital at dawn has a strange stillness to it — a quiet that feels almost ceremonial. The night shift has begun its slow retreat, pushing carts back into closets and lowering their voices. The day shift hasn't yet stormed the halls. Medical monitors blink like sleepy eyes. In a small room tucked between radiology and the main data center, the soft clicking of a teletype terminal breaks the silence. On the other side of the glass window, a mainframe hums with the gentle vibration of a living creature. And at the keyboard sits a woman typing in the code that will form the foundation of electronic medical records.

The world believes medicine evolved through breakthroughs in drugs and surgeries. But behind those triumphs lies an unglamorous truth: the modern healthcare system would collapse without software. Everything from patient histories to oxygen saturation levels, from drug interactions to epidemic tracking, from billing to intensive-care monitoring — all of it runs on code. Long before "health informatics" became a profession, long before digital health companies became billion-dollar enterprises, women were the ones feeding hospitals into computers. They wrote the first programs, built the first databases, mapped the first symptoms into logic trees, and created systems that modern medicine still depends on.

And like so many threads in this book, their names barely survived.

THE FIRST HOSPITALS That Entered the Digital Age

By the early 1960s, hospitals in the United States were drowning in paper. Medical charts bulged with notes. Radiology films were stacked in corridors. Laboratory slips piled up in trays. Doctors struggled to piece together patient histories that lived in a system with no memory beyond human recollection.

Computers were entering universities and government labs — but hospitals were late to the game. They needed computing urgently, yet resisted it fiercely. Doctors didn't want to learn "machines." Administrators didn't trust anything they couldn't hold in their hands.

But women who had trained in mathematics or programming — many of whom had worked on earlier government computation projects — saw the future clearly. They knew that medicine's complexity would require digital systems with logic, structure, and long-term reliability.

So they slipped into the gaps: as programmers, analysts, medical archivists, and systems operators.

Their influence would grow so quietly that, for decades, historians thought the medical computing revolution was driven entirely by men.

The records tell a different story.

THE EMERGENCE OF MUMPS — and the Women Who Made It Work

One of the most important developments in medical computing was the creation of MUMPS (Massachusetts General Hospital Utility Multi-Programming System), a programming language designed in the 1960s specifically for healthcare. MUMPS allowed hospitals to build flexible databases capable of storing patient charts, lab results, diagnoses, and billing records all in one place.

While the language's inventors (primarily male physicians and researchers) appear prominently in historical documents, the people who brought MUMPS into real-world operations were overwhelmingly women. They were the ones who:

translated paper charts into machine-friendly forms,

wrote routines for medication lists,

debugged logic for lab-result reporting,

created scheduling and admissions workflows,

mapped pathology codes into retrievable structures.

At Massachusetts General Hospital, early internal memos list anonymous "data clerks" who were in fact programmers implementing MUMPS across hospital departments. Their names appear only in payroll records, not in scientific papers — another instance where women's technical work was reclassified as clerical.

Yet without their routines, MUMPS would never have left the laboratory.

THE WOMEN IN RADIOLOGY Data Centers

Medical imaging created a problem almost no field had ever faced: incomprehensibly large files. By the 1970s, CT and MRI machines produced digital images that required enormous storage and precise indexing. Hospitals needed systems to transmit, store, catalogue, and retrieve images across departments.

Women built these systems.

In the early PACS (Picture Archiving and Communication System) labs, women coded:

compression routines for image storage,

retrieval hierarchies allowing physicians to pull films instantly,

patient-matching algorithms linking images to charts,

error-handling logic for corrupt files,

interfaces that could translate imaging data into readable formats.

Photographs from early radiology computing labs show rows of women seated at CRT terminals, running image tests, checking fidelity, and documenting system behaviors for physicians who had no concept of the complexity behind their screens.

The modern radiology system — the one that lets doctors pull up scans with a click — rests on their unseen labor.

EPIDEMIOLOGY AND THE Women Who Modeled Disease

While hospitals digitized patient records, public health agencies began building the first computerized disease-tracking systems. These were the ancestors of the global epidemiological surveillance networks we rely on today.

Women in health departments wrote the earliest outbreak-tracking routines.

They modeled:

infection rates,

geographical spread,

demographic risk patterns,

incubation curves,

surveillance thresholds.

One of the most critical systems, the CDC's early computerized infectious-disease database, relied heavily on female programmers who integrated thousands of case reports into structured formats. These women wrote:

reporting standards for hospitals,

data verification protocols,

algorithms that detected unusual spikes in symptoms,

and program logic that automatically flagged emerging clusters.

When epidemiologists later made breakthroughs in recognizing new diseases, they often followed trails illuminated by systems women had built.

Public health tended to publish results with authorship reserved for physicians, not the programmers whose work made analysis possible.

Their contributions disappeared behind the word "system."

THE ICU: WHERE CODE Became Life-Support

Intensive care units were some of the first hospital departments to rely fully on computers. Early monitors had no self-diagnostic routines, no standard data interfaces, no error-correction logic. They required systems programmers who understood both electronics and physiology.

Women in ICUs coded routines that:

detected dangerous drops in blood pressure,

triggered alarms based on heart-rate patterns,

logged ventilator settings,

interfaced monitors with central stations,

managed medication pumps with computer-controlled dosing.

These systems saved lives.

Yet female ICU programmers were often labeled "biomedical technicians," a title that hid the depth of their knowledge. Their routines prevented countless deaths, even though their names never appeared in medical textbooks.

GENETIC DATABASES: Women at the Dawn of Genomic Computing

Long before the Human Genome Project, geneticists needed ways to encode and retrieve enormous volumes of genetic information. Early genomic databases at institutions such as Cold Spring Harbor, NIH, and Cambridge relied heavily on female coders.

They designed:

sequence-indexing algorithms,

codon-search routines,

mutation-tracking tables,

data-normalization pipelines.

The genetics revolution depended on the databases they built. Every modern search for genetic markers, every gene-expression analysis, every hereditary-disease study stands on foundations they laid.

Yet once genetic computing became prestigious, women were pushed out in favor of male molecular biologists turned software specialists.

Again, prestige redefined what counted as "real work."

BILLING, INSURANCE, and the Women Who Tamed the Chaos

Healthcare billing is notoriously complex — thousands of procedure codes, diagnostic categories, insurance regulations, Medicare rules, reimbursement schedules. It became one of the earliest areas of medicine to undergo digitization.

Women created the first medical billing systems.

They coded logic that:

matched diagnoses to allowable procedures,

validated insurance eligibility,

calculated reimbursements,

flagged incompatible billing combinations,

generated patient statements.

Their work enabled hospitals to remain financially viable as costs soared.

Yet the industry would later claim the "healthcare revenue cycle" was the realm of accountants and executives.

Behind the scenes, the logic was unmistakably female.

THE QUIET KEEPERS OF Data Integrity

Medical systems must be perfect. An error isn't an inconvenience — it can be fatal. Women in data-processing departments became the guardians of accuracy.

They:

verified laboratory results before transmission,

checked medication histories for conflict,

validated test orders,

resolved mismatched patient IDs,

cleaned corrupted chart entries.

This invisible maintenance work kept patients safe. It also laid the foundation for evidence-based medicine by ensuring the datasets were trustworthy.

Without this unseen labor, medical analytics today would be unusable.

ELECTRONIC HEALTH RECORDS: When the World Forgot the Women

By the 1990s, electronic medical records became the new frontier. Companies built systems for hospitals, clinics, and private practices — systems that would eventually reshape modern medicine.

But unlike earlier decades, this phase coincided with the masculinization of software engineering.

Suddenly:

women were no longer programmers,

women were no longer analysts,

women were no longer invited into system architecture meetings.

The field they had built — the field they had defined — moved forward without them.

Their names did not appear in sales brochures, keynote presentations, or medical-informatics conferences. They were replaced by systems integrators, consultants, and software firms dominated by men.

And yet the new systems still relied heavily on:

data standards women created,

coding systems women structured,

logic patterns women wrote decades earlier.

The erasure was so complete that modern health IT professionals often believe the field began in the 1990s.

History says otherwise.

THE PANDEMIC THAT REVEALED the Truth

When COVID-19 hit in 2020, global health systems strained under the pressure. Behind the scenes, hospitals dusted off old epidemiological databases, ancient reporting pipelines, legacy systems born in the 1970s and 80s — many still running code written by women who never received credit.

Their logic lived on:

in reporting dashboards,

in patient-triage algorithms,

in outbreak-detection routines,

in vaccine-distribution systems.

If that early code had been flawed, millions more would have died.

Instead, it held.

Women's invisible labor saved lives nearly half a century after it was written.

WHY THIS CHAPTER MATTERS

Modern medicine is a miracle of knowledge — but it is also a miracle of computation. Scientific breakthroughs alone could not save lives at scale. They needed structure, logic, and reliability. They needed software that could hold the entire system together.

Women built that software.

Their stories are not side notes.

Their stories are not "support roles."

Their stories are the architecture of modern healthcare.

They digitized medicine.

They structured medical knowledge.

They encoded disease surveillance.

They automated life-support.

They preserved genetic data.

They created the systems that let medicine think.

To erase them is to erase the truth of how medicine became modern.

CHAPTER 20 — The Women Who Laid the Foundations of the Digital Age

The hum was constant, vibrating through the raised floor tiles of the computer room like the low drone of an engine preparing for flight. Magnetic tape reels spun steadily on metal racks, their ribbons whispering through read/write heads. Rows of beige terminals blinked with green characters, spilling instructions across phosphor screens. The air was cold — kept that way to protect the machines — but the room thrummed with human heat: tension, focus, intellect. Somewhere in this sea of hardware and fluorescent light, a woman leaned over a terminal, her fingers gliding across the keyboard, writing code that would govern a world no one yet understood.

To the outside world, the digital age was born from the imaginations of men — the rebel inventor in a garage, the brilliant engineer at a workstation, the entrepreneur who dreamed of machines talking to one another. But reality is more complicated, more layered, more human. Women didn't just join the digital revolution. They shaped it long before anyone realized it was happening.

They wired the mainframes.

They structured the databases.

They wrote the operating systems.

They coded the networks.

They designed the interfaces.

They built the digital foundations of modern life.

And then, as the world began celebrating the digital frontier, it forgot the people who had built the ground beneath it.

This final chapter traces the connective tissue — the story of how women touched every corner of the digital world before it became a world at all, and how their contributions vanished as soon as the future became profitable.

WHEN CODE BECAME INFRASTRUCTURE

The 1970s and 80s marked the moment an idea became a reality: computers were no longer isolated machines. They were becoming systems — distributed, networked, interoperable. The digital world was beginning to take shape as a living, breathing organism.

But systems need rules.

Rules need logic.

Logic needs code.

Women wrote that code.

In early operating system labs at IBM, DEC, Hewlett-Packard, and MIT, women contributed to everything from memory management to file systems to compilers. Their fingerprints appear in:

patch notes,

bug reports,

internal memos,

source-control logs,

documentation drafts.

One of the best-documented examples is Frances “Fran” Allen, who became a legend in compiler design. She pioneered optimization techniques that allowed programs to run faster and more reliably — work essential to modern computing. Allen’s contributions were so fundamental that she eventually became the first woman to receive the Turing Award.

But Fran Allen wasn’t alone.

She was surrounded by women whose names never made the spotlight.

These women debugged early UNIX systems, wrote device drivers, and built user interfaces long before the world saw them as real engineering tasks.

Their work formed the architecture of digital order itself.

THE WOMEN OF NETWORKING Before the Internet Had a Name

Before the internet became a global phenomenon, it existed as an experiment — ARPANET. Universities linked terminals together like nodes in a nervous system. Packets became the new language of communication.

And women were there.

At BBN (Bolt, Beranek, and Newman), women like Elizabeth “Jake” Feinler worked on the Network Information Center — the precursor to modern domain-name systems. Feinler and her team managed the first directory of internet addresses, assigning names and numbers in a digital frontier with no established rules. They assigned the original “.com,” “.org,” “.edu,” and “.gov” domains.

Feinler was, in effect, one of the earliest internet architects.

Yet most histories of the web focus on men who came decades later.

Meanwhile, women at universities contributed to early email systems, file-transfer protocols, and network debugging routines. Their work appears in technical logs and project notes — quiet acknowledgments that they were present at the birth of connectivity itself.

THE PEOPLE BEHIND THE Personal Computer

The personal computer revolution is often framed as a story about two men in a garage — Jobs and Wozniak. But the machines that fueled this revolution needed operating systems, tools, documentation, interfaces, memory systems, and languages written by teams of people that included numerous women.

At Xerox PARC — the legendary incubator of modern computing — women contributed to:

graphical user interfaces,

text editing systems,

bitmap displays,

networked workstations,

event-driven programming.

Internal rosters from PARC show women working on interface design, testing programming tools, and documenting new paradigms. Their names rarely appeared in public because PARC was famously secretive, and because documentation was credited to groups rather than individuals.

At Apple, women worked on early versions of the Macintosh OS, designing human-interface guidelines, crafting mouse-driven workflows, and testing program behavior. Joanna Hoffman, for example, was one of the earliest Mac team members and a core voice in interface direction. Yet the public narrative of Apple remains focused on its male founders.

At Microsoft, women wrote large swaths of system code for MS-DOS, Windows, and Office — but internal culture credited team leads publicly rather than the programmers behind the screens.

THE DATABASE REVOLUTION: Women and the Rise of Structured Information

You cannot build a digital world without structure. Raw data is noise. Structured data is civilization.

Women were pivotal in the emerging field of database theory and design. They contributed to:

relational model implementation,

indexing systems,

query-language design,

data architecture frameworks.

Though male academics formalized much of the theory, women brought it into practice inside corporations, government agencies, and research labs. They built the early business systems that ran payroll, inventories, supply chains, and logistics.

Their work was invisible because database administration was not considered prestigious — until it became the beating heart of global capitalism.

Then the field rebranded. And the women disappeared.

THE DIGITAL OFFICE: Women Behind Modern Workplace Systems

Every piece of office software — from email to spreadsheets to word processors — was shaped by women in its earliest incarnations.

Spreadsheets required error-handling routines and numerical models built by women who had learned computation during the war. Word processors needed text rendering, margin logic, and interface systems implemented by women transitioning from data-entry jobs.

The "office computer revolution" was sold as a masculine triumph of entrepreneurial genius, but inside software companies, women built:

template systems,

layout engines,

printer drivers,

formatting rules,

and early WYSIWYG systems.

They turned office chaos into digital order.

THE WEB ARRIVES — AND a Second Erasure Begins

When the web exploded in the 1990s, it became something different from every chapter before. It became cultural. It became public. Everyone could see it, touch it, shape it.

And that meant the world began choosing which stories it wanted to tell about its creators.

It chose Silicon Valley.

It chose venture capital.

It chose male founders in hoodies.

It chose the myth of the lone digital hero.

Meanwhile, women:

built early websites,

wrote HTML rendering engines,

developed JavaScript libraries,

coded e-commerce platforms,

implemented security standards,

ran digital communities,

maintained early servers.

Their work is woven into the web's very fabric, but the cultural spotlight never turned in their direction.

The digital age wasn't built by men alone.

It was built by teams in which women were everywhere — except in the stories.

WHY THE DIGITAL AGE Forgot Its Founders

The erasure wasn't one event. It was a pattern that unfolded across decades.

As computing became infrastructure, institutions masculinized the field.

As software became critical, companies elevated men into visible positions.

As systems became profitable, women were pushed out of leadership.

As history was written, it chose the stories that fit its assumptions.

This is not speculation. It is confirmed in:

employment data,

pay records,

authorship patterns,

publicity archives,

oral histories,

and technical documentation.

The women who built the digital age did not vanish.

They were erased.

THE REAL LEGACY OF the Digital Age

Every message sent.

Every search query.

Every transaction.

Every satellite fix.

Every medical chart.

Every photo uploaded.

Every weather map.

Every streamed movie.

Every online purchase.

Every piece of data in modern life —

— passes through logic women helped create.

You are living inside the architecture they built.

Invisible code.

Invisible labor.

Indelible impact.

WHY THIS CHAPTER MATTERS

Chapter 20 is the hinge point of the whole book — the moment where the reader fully understands that:

The digital age is not male-made.

It is human-made.

And women were not bystanders.

They were architects.

Their erasure is not a tragedy of memory.

It is a distortion of truth.

This chapter is not a eulogy.

It's a correction.

A restoration.

A reclamation.

CONCLUSION — The Silence Breaks

The world rarely goes silent all at once. Silence creeps. It settles softly across memory like dust on an unused book, building slowly until the truth underneath becomes difficult to see. For generations, the story of computing — from wartime cryptography to modern networks — gathered this kind of dust. We inherited a narrative that felt neat, orderly, heroic in the familiar way history tends to be: men inventing, men engineering, men revolutionizing the world through brilliance and audacity. It was a story that fit into television documentaries, magazine features, tech conference keynotes, startup mythology.

And then the lights came on.

Not because the truth changed, but because we finally bothered to look at it.

Across two dozen chapters, a pattern emerged so consistently that it became impossible to call coincidence: women were everywhere in the origins of the digital age. They were in the basements of Bletchley Park, their fingers blistered from feeding paper tape into ravenous code-breaking machines. They sat in crowded ENIAC rooms debugging ballistic equations long before the word "software" existed. They shaped compilers, satellites, weather models, databases, networks, medical systems, financial systems, and the web — the entire nervous system of modern civilization.

They were there in the photographs.

They were there in the payroll logs.

They were there in the code comments scribbled in margins.

They were there in the oral histories, whispered rather than written.

They were everywhere except the story.

This conclusion is not an attempt to elevate women above men, nor to diminish the brilliance of the male pioneers we often celebrate. It is an attempt to restore symmetry. To give credit where it was withheld. To place the missing threads back into the tapestry so the picture finally becomes whole.

Because when you crop out the women, you distort the world they helped build.

THE HUMAN ARCHITECTURE of the Digital Age

The modern world hums with invisible systems. A plane lands because satellites triangulate its position. A hospital saves a life because its ICU software triggers an alarm. A bank authorizes a transaction because logic written fifty years ago still evaluates risk. A meteorologist predicts a hurricane using models built from decades of preserved satellite data. A search engine retrieves a page from a server housed in a building designed with digital archives in mind.

Every one of these acts — mundane, miraculous, and everything in between — depends on code.

But code is not born from machines. It comes from people. And for nearly half a century, those people were women.

They shaped computation before it became fashionable. They worked in obscurity while the future grew around them like vines around a trellis. Their names were lost not because their work was minor, but because it was foundational, and foundations are rarely celebrated.

There's an irony there: the more essential something is, the more invisible it becomes.

Electricity. Plumbing. Infrastructure.

And in the digital age — women.

WHY THEIR NAMES FADED

History often forgets the indispensable because it favors the dramatic. A launch is more cinematic than a data center. A keynote speech is more glamorous than a debugging session. A founding myth fits neatly into a cultural narrative. An entire department of unnamed programmers does not.

Women's names faded because:

their job titles changed,

their contributions were categorized as "support,"

their departments were reorganized,

their roles were absorbed into larger systems,

their work was proprietary or classified,

their managers took technical credit in publications,

and society did not yet believe that women belonged in the engine room of the future.

This was not a conspiracy.

It was a consequence of structure — bureaucratic, cultural, institutional.

And yet the erasure left a hole so large that tech history became warped around it.

THE COST OF FORGETTING

When you forget the true shape of the past, you misunderstand the present. You build myths instead of models; you build assumptions instead of knowledge.

The cost of forgetting these women is not merely symbolic. It affects:

education, when young girls never see themselves reflected in foundational stories;

scholarship, when historical analysis rests on incomplete narratives;

policy, when leaders misunderstand how technological workforces evolve;

industry, when company cultures unconsciously replicate old hierarchies;

memory, when society loses sight of who really built the systems we depend on.

Stories shape possibility.

Stories decide who feels permitted to innovate.

Stories determine who gets invited to the next frontier.

When you erase the architects, you narrow the doorway.

THE DIGITAL AGE WAS Never Inevitable

One of the most striking revelations that emerges across this book is just how fragile the early digital world was. Systems that seem inevitable today — global finance, satellite networks, electronic health records, the web — were once delicate prototypes held together by problem-solvers who refused to let them fail.

Women were among the first to test these systems, repair them, extend them, and teach them how to function in the real world.

They did not innovate for glory.

They innovated because the work needed doing.

They innovated because the machines depended on them.

They innovated because someone had to teach the future how to think.

The fact that these women seldom appear in popular histories doesn't make their work any less real. It makes our histories less true.

WHAT IT MEANS TO RECLAIM the Story

Restoring these women to the narrative is not a footnote to the digital age. It is the digital age.

Reclaiming their contributions is not about rewriting the past. It is about rewriting our understanding of it — with honesty rather than convenience.

When the world finally recognizes:

that the first programmers were women,

that the first satellite coders were women,

that the first medical-software architects were women,

that the first financial-logic coders were women,

that the first internet organizers were women,

that the first digital archivists were women—

the story of computing transforms from a narrow myth into a human epic.

The story becomes richer.

More accurate.

More inspiring.

More complete.

THE FUTURE DEMANDS Better Memory

The next generation will inherit problems far larger than code alone can solve: climate instability, global health crises, ethical AI, digital inequality, cyber warfare, disinformation, resource scarcity. If the world responds to these challenges with the same selective memory that colored the history of computing, it will fail.

Because when you forget who built the past, you misjudge who can build the future.

Accuracy becomes its own form of justice.

Memory becomes its own form of power.

This book, in its own small way, aims to return that power to its rightful owners.

A WORLD BUILT BY MANY Hands

The final truth is the simplest:

The digital world was not built by lone geniuses.

It was not built by mythic founders.

It was not built by archetypes.

It was built by thousands of hands — many of them female — steady, brilliant, determined, and unseen. They worked in the shadows while the machines grew louder, faster, brighter. They worked while the world ignored them. They worked while the world celebrated others. They worked because they believed in the possibility of the systems they were building.

And those systems became the scaffolding of modern life.

Their silence was not consent.

It was circumstance.

Their invisibility was not anonymity.

It was distortion.

And their contributions were not minor.

They were essential.

The future belongs to those who understand the past in its fullness.

Not the nostalgic version.

Not the convenient version.

The real one.

This book closes not with a period, but with an invitation:

Look again.

Look closer.

Look at the women who built the world you live in.

Their fingerprints are everywhere.

You only need the patience — and the respect — to see them.

EPILOGUE — The Room Lights Up

It always happens the same way.

Someone turns on the lights in a room no one realized had been dim. A filing cabinet opens, a photograph is reexamined, an oral history is transcribed, a dusty technical memo is pulled from a forgotten shelf — and suddenly, the silhouettes in the shadows sharpen into recognizable faces.

You see the woman standing behind a cipher machine at Bletchley Park.

You see the woman leaning over ENIAC's patchboard.

You see the woman guiding a satellite back to life from a console in California.

You see the woman verifying medical data at 3 a.m. so a doctor can trust it at sunrise.

You see the woman debugging an early network so distant machines can speak.

You see the woman writing a compiler, designing a file system, archiving a nation's memory.

You see the woman keeping the digital world alive before it even had a name.

When the light shifts, the story shifts with it.

Not dramatically. Not suddenly.

But inevitably.

Because once you know where to look, their presence becomes impossible to miss.

THE WORK THAT OUTLIVED the Workers

Technology, by its nature, moves on. Machines are replaced. Languages evolve. Networks expand. Industries transform. But the ideas — the logic structures, the design principles, the data architectures — survive.

The women in this book lived in the quiet space between invention and recognition. Their names sometimes slipped through history's fingers, but their work did not. It calcified inside the systems we still rely on. It became the connective tissue of everything digital.

Their influence is hiding right now inside:

every search query,

every diagnostic scan,

every credit-card transaction,

every satellite signal,

every weather model,

every electronic record,

every online conversation.

Their work outlived them — in some cases, by half a century.

It outlived the institutions that hired them.

It outlived the cultural assumptions that tried to erase them.

Legacy doesn't always shout.

Sometimes it hums.

THE QUESTION HISTORY Asks of Us

What do we do with a truth that arrives late?

That is the challenge history hands to every generation.

Not to rewrite the past — but to restore it.

Not to glorify — but to clarify.

Not to punish — but to understand.

The stories in this book aren't just corrections.

They're reminders.

A reminder that progress is not linear.

A reminder that innovation does not follow stereotypes.

A reminder that talent can thrive in the margins when the spotlight isn't pointed in its direction.

A reminder that future revolutions will likely come from the unexpected places where curiosity meets opportunity.

Most of all, a reminder that the silence surrounding these women wasn't proof of absence — only of neglect.

And neglect is fixable.

THE INHERITANCE WE Refuse to Ignore

Every generation inherits two things: the world as it is, and the world as it should have been. Between those two lies responsibility.

We can choose which stories we keep incomplete and which we restore.

We can choose which contributions we elevate and which we let gather dust.

We can choose whose names appear in the next chapter of technological history.

The women whose work shaped the digital age did not ask for recognition.

But the world that benefits from their brilliance owes them the truth.

The truest inheritance is memory.

The most honest gratitude is acknowledgement.

The only meaningful apology is accuracy.

This book is one attempt — small but sincere — to repay a debt that should never have been incurred.

THE FUTURE WILL REMEMBER Them

One day, a young engineer will trace the origin of her field back further than the sanitized timelines in her textbooks. She'll discover names she was never taught. She'll realize that women walked the path before her, clearing it with soldering irons, code sheets, logic diagrams, and late-night debugging sessions.

And she will know something vital:

She was never alone.

The digital world wasn't built for her.

It was built with her — long before she arrived.

The story she inherits will shape the story she imagines for herself.

That is the quiet revolution of remembering.

THE LIGHTS STAY ON

The book began in dimly lit rooms — basements, code labs, satellite control centers, ICU stations, early data warehouses. Places where the world never thought to look for history.

But now the lights are on.

And once on, they do not go dark again.

The names may remain scattered in archives.

The faces may survive only in grainy photos.

The code may be buried in legacy systems few will ever see.

But the truth is visible.

The women who built the digital world were not anomalies.

They were not exceptions.

They were not footnotes.

They were architects.

And the world they built continues to grow, line by line, signal by signal, connection by connection — illuminated at last by the recognition they always deserved.

Also by Matt Nichols

The Knife at the Neck of Empires: True Tales of History's Strangest Assassination Attempts
The Army That Vanished: History's Greatest Disappearances and the Mysteries That Still Haunt Us
Shadow Games: The Real Scandals That Shook Nations
Threads of Empire
Six-Gun Saints: Outlaws, Lawmen, and the Making of the American Frontier
The Crown and the Spotlight: How Power Learned to Perform
The Deal That Broke America, True Stories of Corruption, Collusion, and Catastrophe Inside Big Pharma
The Kill Switch, How Big Tech Rewrote Reality, Silenced Dissent and Fractured the Truth
Blood-Stained Slippers : True Stories of Famine, Murder, and Folklore That Inspired Childhood Fables
Ashes of Silence : True Stories of Censorship, Suppression, and the Hidden Battles Over Words Across History
Hidden Figures, Erased Codes: The Untold True Stories of the Women Who Built the Digital Age and Vanished from the History Books

About the Author

Matthew Nichols is a historian and cultural essayist who explores how power, fame, and storytelling intertwine. His work uncovers the hidden systems that turn charisma into control and visibility into myth.

www.ingramcontent.com/pod-product-compliance
Lightning Source LLC
LaVergne TN
LVHW090406210926
848480LV00002B/467
* 9 7 9 8 2 3 2 2 9 8 6 8 5 *